ANN JAMIESON

FOR THE

LOVE

OF THE

HORSE

VOLUME IV

AMAZING TRUE STORIES ABOUT THE HORSES WE LOVE

**Cover Photo story (Finding Skye)
on page 41**

Animals make people human.
-Unknown

Contents

INTRODUCTION

Anyone who loves horses will appreciate this book.

These are all true stories: stories about the bond between horses and humans. That bond is not particular to one breed or one discipline; it encompasses everyone who spends time in any way with these incredibly generous souls.

I wrote this book to celebrate that bond, to honor the horse. Horses bring so many gifts into our lives in so many ways.

Acknowledgements

A HUGE thank you to Lisa Kelly and David Van Amber, who took time out from their crazy schedules to give me the story of Lisa, Skye, and Rocky, and find those photos!

Thank you to Boyd Martin, Lisa Jacquin, Tony D'Ambrosio, Tom McCutcheon, Sarah Willeman, Tina Konyot, Patti Gruber, and all the other people and horses who shared their stories with me.

Thank you to Diana De Rosa for always providing me with great photos, often at a moment's notice! Thank you to all the other great photographers who have allowed me to use their photos.

Thank you to Robert Goodman who went above and beyond the call of friendship, spending endless hours going through the stories with a fine-tooth comb, and providing great insight into how they could be improved.

And another huge Thank You to Beth Vaculik, who has the unique ability to use both sides of her brain equally well. A superb artist, Beth always knows just what to do to make the books look smashing. As a formatter, she knows how to use technology to our best advantage. Beth, you are amazing! A thousand "Thank-You's"!

DEDICATION

To all horses everywhere,
for all you do for the human race

HEROES

⟶ NEVILLE BARDOS

The first time Boyd Martin saved Neville Bardos' life was when he picked him up for $850 at the racetrack. Three-year-old Neville was headed for slaughter.

Boyd's friend Gordon Bishop had looked at Neville first. Labeling him "no good" as a jumper, he turned him down. Boyd thought otherwise.

Born at Woodlands, a top racing stud in Scone, Northern New South Wales, and sired by Mahaya, a "shuttle stallion" who had been flown over to Australia from the United States for a breeding season, Neville raced ("terribly," says Boyd) at Kemba Grange racetrack.

Neville's owner wanted $1000 for the horse. Boyd bargained him down to $850.

The next day Boyd found out that Neville was a cribber. Furious that the seller had "cheated him," he almost asked for his money back. Almost.

Boyd had purchased Neville as a sales prospect, but he soon discovered that his new horse was rather more fiery than first impressions might have suggested. "I felt," says Boyd, "like he was too wild to sell!" Besides, Boyd had learned that the horse was tough, and could run and jump well, so perhaps there was a future for him with this horse. "In the back of my mind I knew he was an upper level horse."

Neville was also a character with a love for surprising those around him. At one event, Neville was unloaded from the van. As soon as he hit ground, he bolted, wearing his shipping boots, helmet, and halter, and dragging his lead shank behind him. Racing to the competition ring, Neville jumped over a barrier right onto the jumping course, where a competitor was in the midst of their round. It took five people and a lot of time to catch him. Neville's name is well chosen: he is named after a fast talking, hotheaded, stand over gangster who lives in Melbourne.

In his first event, in 2002, Neville tackled the cross-country course with Boyd's wife Silva on board. Silva is a Grand Prix dressage rider from Germany, who now rides for the United States. Silva fell off on course and Neville took off, running for about 15 minutes before he was finally caught. Remounting, Silva finished the course. The clock had not been stopped so Neville's penalty points were impressive, "about 480," declares Boyd.

But in 2006 Neville went on to win the Coffs Harbor CIC** and the Melbourne CCI**. Boyd never let Gordon live down his initial evaluation of Neville. He wasted no opportunity to take his "no good" jumper's ribbons, and place them in Gordon's tack room at every event Neville placed in.

In order to import and compete his mercurial rising star, Boyd formed the Neville Bardos Syndicate, which now owns the horse. This allowed Neville and Boyd to move to the United States in 2007. (Boyd now maintains dual citizenship). In their first CCI*** at Jersey Fresh they ran 11th. In the fall of that year, they placed fourth at Fair Hill. The following year, they placed ninth at Rolex Kentucky, their first four star, short listing them for the Beijing Olympics and honoring Boyd with the Carimati Cup for the highest placed foreign rider.

When they returned to Fair Hill in 2009, Neville was just coming back from an injury. He had only one Preliminary under his belt in preparation for the three star event. Fair Hill perfectly spotlighted Neville's rugged character. "The conditions were horrible, with monsoon conditions and mud up to their knees. Neville won by a huge margin of nine or 10 points. He's so tough he was the only one to be within the time," Boyd states proudly. "He always rises to the occasion. As the courses get tougher and more technical, that's when we see him at his best. When the going gets tough, Nev gets going."

Boyd likens Neville's personality to "a bouncer at a nightclub, on amphetamines. He's always looking for action, he loves his work, loves being part of the excitement."

In 2010 Neville competed in the World Equestrian Games in Kentucky, finishing 10th, and laying claim to the title of the highest placed horse from the United States.

After the highs of the previous years, 2011 turned into a year of heart-breaking disaster and loss. In May, the barn in Pennsylvania that they leased from Phillip Dutton burned, killing six horses and drastically injuring others.

Boyd risked his life (as did Phillip Dutton) to save the horses. He says, "About 150 firemen were standing around, watching the barn burn. It was a bit of a surreal experience. I felt helpless; I had to do something." Although the fire chief told Boyd he couldn't go in, fearing the roof was in danger of imminent collapse, Boyd "bolted in. I had no idea where I was, where I was going. I didn't go in after Neville; I just went in. I heard a horse gurgling, groaning. He was quivering in a corner."

It was Neville. Boyd grabbed him by his cribbing collar. As he attempted to pull him out, "Phillip appears like a ghost out of nowhere. He pushed from behind as I pulled in front."

The cribbing that almost caused Boyd to pass Neville by was now the saving grace that allowed his rescue. And Boyd had saved Neville's life for the second time.

Neville went straight down the road to New Bolton. The "blood work" was disastrous. Basically, Neville should be dead. "It was devastating, the equivalent of a horse about to die. He had horrible smoke inhalation, and burns on his skin, burns through his windpipe and esophagus." No one knew if he would survive.

Yet Neville was standing in the stall, eating his hay. The horse the vets were looking at didn't match the blood work. The vets didn't know how to approach him, what to do. They had never confronted anything like this. Any horse this badly burned would be dead.

The veterinarians were forced to consult human burn centers at hospitals to compare injuries and determine a course of treatment.

Despite his life-threatening injuries, Neville's recovery followed a course that was nothing short of miraculous. He seemed to know he would be just fine. "He had a good look in his eye, and he never went off his feed."

Neville lived in a hyperbaric chamber at Fair Hill Therapy for an hour a day for two weeks. The chamber made a huge difference, greatly improving the health of his lungs and the condition of the burns on his skin. Boyd is tremendously appreciative of Dr. Kevin Kane and the Fair Hill Therapy team for all their help.

At one point Boyd mentioned to the vets that Neville had a shot at the Olympics next year. Their immediate reply? "Not a chance."

The eventing community poured out their support to the Martins. Bruce Davidson came to the farm and was, for once, speechless, when he surveyed the ruins. Jimmy Wofford called. Fundraisers were organized by Karen O'Connor, the Carolina Horse Park, Fernanda Kellogg of Fitch's Corner in Millbrook, New York, and the Martins' sponsor, Ecogold.

But the fire turned out to be only the beginning.

While still overwhelmed by the fear and heartbreak of that horrific night, Boyd got the news that his father had been killed while riding his bicycle in Australia. Then Silva's father in Germany died of cancer.

The Martins were inconsolable. Their world was upside down; they seemed to be losing everything.

Everything that is, except a spunky little ex-racehorse.

Neville was recovering brilliantly. The vets were astounded by his progress, labeling it as "nothing less than a miracle."

Boyd had always dreamed of competing at the World Equestrian Games. Neville had not only taken him there, he had taken him to the best placed finish for the U.S. team. Boyd also dreamed of competing at Burghley, one of the toughest four stars on the face of the earth.

Tentatively, Boyd circled the date on his calendar. It was only two months away. Ordinarily, it takes 12-16 weeks to prepare a horse for a four star. Boyd states, "It's my job to gauge and feel where my horses are at." Neville was feeling good.

It was a "calculated, but educated gamble to bring him back for Burghley." Day by day, Boyd looked at his horse, at what he was riding every time he sat on his back.

The horse was taking his mind off of his crushing losses, giving him instead something positive to focus on. It was much better for Neville to be galloping up hills than to stay at New Bolton in the critical care unit. Boyd says, "It was good for both of us to be out and doing something."

Phillip's support was crucial. While everyone else was hemming and hawing as to whether shooting for Burghley was a good idea, Phillip said, "Yes, you can do this. This is a realistic decision."

Worried about the lack of time, Boyd wonders if he "over-did it. I worried so much that he wouldn't be fit enough that I got him too fit."

At one of the preparatory events, the Millbrook Horse Trials in Millbrook, New York, Neville completed in spectacular form, placing fourth in the Advanced division. There was no doubt he was announcing to all that he was ready for Burghley.

In only eight weeks, and coming back from a near fatal fire, Neville was ready for one of the toughest four stars in the world.

Although Neville has never lost his wild, overexuberant side, for the whole week of Burghley he changed: he remained focused and settled. He seemed to realize just what he was facing. The course was mammoth, with a huge ditch and brush that is said to be the biggest cross-country fence in the world.

The world's attention found itself focused not just on the historic event, but on Neville's story, the story of a tenacious little horse that had come back from near-fatal injuries to tackle Burghley.

In dressage Neville scored a 49.7. He made the cross-country course look easy, finishing on his dressage score, and so full of energy that he seemed to be asking if he could do it again. As his groom Lindsey Taylor held him for the farrier after his round so his studs could be removed, Boyd's wife Silva came up to her. Overcome with emotion she said, "He wasn't even supposed to be here, Lindsey."

A single rail in show jumping added 4 faults to his score, putting Neville in seventh place.

Neville fulfilled Boyd's dream of competing at Burghley, bringing him in at a top ten finish. He restored the faith of a family crushed with disaster, putting a horrific summer behind them with his tenacity and bravery. He brought hope and a mission to a family in despair.

Boyd says, "He was never a horse I thought would do everything that he's done; but he's got such heart and that counts more than talent."

The London Olympics loom on the horizon, less than a year away. But for now Boyd is content. His goals for Neville are "just to watch him eat grass and windsuck in the paddock for the next few months."

⟿ SERGEANT RECKLESS

She has her own fan page on Facebook, and her own website. She recently had a two-year-old racehorse named after her, even though she fought in the Korean War and died in 1968. Earning two Purple Hearts, a Good Conduct Medal, National Defense Service Medal, and a Presidential Unit Citation with star, among other military decorations, she was featured in *Life Magazine's* "Celebrating Our Heroes" as one of our country's 100 greatest heroes of all time (along with George Washington and Abraham Lincoln).

Reckless was known for her bravery--and her appetite. She was assigned to carry ammunition to the front lines for the 75 mm Recoilless Rifle Platoon of the 5th Marines. Purchased for $250 by commanding officer Lt. Eric Pederson, the Mongolian mare came from the Seoul Racetrack, and soon proved to be priceless.

Her former owner, young Kim Huk Moon, sold her only because he needed the money to pay for an artificial leg for his sister, Chung Soon, who had lost her leg to a land mine. Reckless originally had been called Flame-in-the-Morning, but the Marines called her Reckless after the nickname for an antitank weapon with a fierce back blast.

Reckless didn't need to be told how important a good breakfast was to start one's day. She lived by that rule. Scrambled eggs and pancakes with her morning cup of coffee were her preferred meal in the morning.

Snacks throughout the day were important. Cake, potato chips, peanut butter and jelly, cola, candy bars, all were high on her list of consumables. But it wasn't just the food that mattered. Reckless demanded attention, and lots of it. If her demands weren't being met, hats, blankets, and even poker chips made it on to the consumable list. One poker game had to be ended prematurely when it was discovered that Reckless had eaten a stack of poker chips.

Reckless wasn't particularly fussy about her glassware: cans, cups, canteens, even helmets would do. The Marines always were happy to share whatever they had to eat or drink with her.

When she wasn't eating, Reckless worked. Carrying rations, grenades, medical supplies, ammunition, and sleeping bags, she earned her pancakes and candy. The steep terrain of Korea was too much for jeeps, but not too much for Reckless. Nimbly navigating the hills, she learned to step over barbed wire, crouch down in foxholes and to head for a bunker when she heard incoming rounds.

The Marines quickly grew to love Reckless both for her bravery and her goofy character, often allowing the pony sized mare (at 14.1 hands) to sleep in their tents with them, shielding her with their flak jackets to protect her.

Reckless is best known for her service during the Battle of Outpost Vegas in March of 1953, one of the most ferocious battles of the war. This five day battle saw Reckless on one day alone make 51 trips from the Ammunition Supply Point to the firing sites, 95% of the time by *herself*. Carrying nearly five *tons* of ammunition over the course of the battle, the little sorrel mare walked over 35 miles through open rice paddies and up steep mountains with enemy rounds constantly peppering her. Reckless would carry ammo up the mountain, get unloaded, and then carry wounded Marines down the mountain.

An infantryman who was one of only two to make it off of "Hill Vegas" alive, Harold Wadley remembers seeing Reckless coming up the ridge. "Generally one Marine led Reckless and she brought up ammo. Some of the gun crew were wounded, so they didn't have an extra Marine. She made that trip all night long by herself. They would tie a wounded Marine on her and turn her around and she'd head down that ridge with all this artillery and mortar coming in. The guys down there would unload the wounded off her and the ammo on her and she would turn around right on her own and head right back up. She knew exactly what her job was."

Reckless delivered critical ammunition under constant fire, performing her work in a human capacity, unguided by anything but her own enormous desire to serve. The number of lives she saved can't be counted, and the appearance of the little chestnut mare with the bright white stripe guaranteed a boost in morale.

Her selfless service in this battle not only earned her the respect of all those around her, but also got her promoted to Staff Sergeant, a title never before or since bestowed upon an animal. After all, her courage and dedication to duty defined the word "Marine."

Wounded twice during the battle, Reckless never stopped. She continued to see further action during the war. After the signing of the truce in July the Marines traveled home, but Reckless, mired in bureaucratic red tape, was left behind. It wasn't until the *Saturday Evening Post* ran an article about her in April 1954 that people became aware of her plight. In response, Reckless was offered free transportation on a shipping line by an executive of the line who had read the article. She landed in San Francisco on November 10, 1954.

In retirement Reckless served as mascot of the 1st Marine Division. She attended retirements, promotions, birthdays, and civilian parades. The order had been given that, in recognition of all Sergeant Reckless had done, there was never to be more weight on her back again than a blanket. That order stood. When Reckless went on her daily jog at Camp Pendleton, the Marine who accompanied her did so on foot.

Reckless had four foals, three of whom continued to live with her at Camp Pendleton: Dauntless, Fearless and Chesty. One filly died sadly at only a month old.

Reckless died at the age of 20, and is buried at Camp Pendleton where a monument to her stands at Stepp Stables. But her story is just beginning.

A YouTube video (http://youtu.be/YIo3ZfA9da0) has garnered hundreds of thousands of views, a new book is being written, and a movie and a monument in or near the Korean War Memorial are being planned. This game little mare was an inspiration to all those who knew her, and her story will continue to inspire all those who didn't.

Check out her fan page (Official Sgt. Reckless Fan Club) or website www.sgtreckless.com and be sure to read the book *Sgt. Reckless* when it comes out.

⟶ You Have to Learn the Art

Donna Ponessa's love affair with horses began when she was nine years old. Trading riding lessons for work at a local barn, she soon progressed to riding and showing horses for others, and competing in the hunter/ jumper divisions.

In 1982 Donna was diagnosed with Multiple Sclerosis. She continued her education, graduating and beginning work as a Registered Nurse. Donna also purchased a horse of her own, Remington Steele. She discovered Remington in a field, and he was at the time so ugly that his nickname became "Ugh." Later on, though, he morphed into "an absolute swan" and his nickname became simply Remy.

Sadly, Donna's MS progressed within two years to where she was in a wheelchair, and found herself hospitalized every six months for treatment. Unable to work, she was forced to sell Remy. That, says Donna, "was a really, really dark period, one of the darkest periods in my life."

In addition to not being able to afford Remy, she was also unable to ride him. A cold-backed horse, it was very difficult for him to stand still long enough for Donna to mount. He was also unable to deal with her inconstant balance, and Donna found herself hitting the dirt far too often. The decision to sell him was heartbreaking, "It was one of the hardest things I've ever had to do."

Donna didn't believe she would ever ride again.

A year later, she was able to return to work. Throughout her life Donna had been an athlete, and kept herself fit and strong. Although she would have loved to ride again, her perception of disabled riders was that of the ones she had seen in therapeutic riding programs. The riders were led around the ring with side-walkers on each side. "That's not riding," she thought. She wasn't interested.

Since riding wasn't an option, she looked for an outlet for her competitive drive. She found it with competitive wheelchair tennis, achieving a national ranking of #2.

By 1993, Donna needed a power wheelchair, a tracheostomy to breathe, and had had to undergo aggressive chemotherapy to slow the disease process. The chemo was used in order to eradicate the white blood cells, which contained an abnormal protein. The hope was that when new white cells were produced, they wouldn't be as abnormal.

Donna's severely compromised health meant she could no longer play tennis.

In 2001 she was able to return to work. A few years later, Donna saw some photos of "para-riding," and thought it looked cool. She made a deal with herself. If she got herself off the ventilator, she would let herself ride again.

It took her two years to get off the ventilator enough to go back to riding. Donna's diaphragm has severely limited function, so she needed to develop other muscles to help her breathe. By constantly working out she strengthened her back muscles and intercostals (those that surround the rib cage) so that she could use them to breathe. Meanwhile, her nurses took her off her ventilator a little at a time, for short periods, so she could develop the ability to function without it.

Donna attributes her ability to return to riding to a combination of very aggressive treatment, and her commitment to being in great physical shape. She was so strong, that she was able to endure a lot of things that would knock other people out. Although many people who live with MS are advised to take it easy and rest, Donna knows that she has survived her illness because she has always kept herself fit.

When she finally got back on a horse, Donna says, "It was surreal. I couldn't believe I was actually there. I just wanted to make time stand still. I can still recall all the details: the smell of the barn, what I was wearing, the horse, the instructor, the ring…"

Donna rode with Susan Stegmeyer, who initially walked beside her before letting her walk unassisted. Then she let Donna trot a little, with the horse on a lunge line.

Although that first ride was "like a celebration," after that, "reality set in. Riding now was very, very different."

The former jumper rider who was used to hot horses, tiny saddles, and using her legs and hands for communication now had very little sensation below the breastbone. She had no way to communicate with her legs. Sometimes she felt like "a head bobbing in the air above the horse. It was extremely frustrating, not at all like it used to be." Although glad to be riding again, Donna says it was "a little bittersweet."

Donna would think her body was doing one thing, but when she looked in the mirror, "It was totally different." *How do I communicate now,* she wondered? *I have no use of my legs.* Later on, Donna's research on the Internet revealed that the communication of the legs is replaced by using two whips.

Donna's grief over losing her former ability to ride was helped immensely by Susan's advice. "You have to enjoy the journey. Just keep your eyes on the prize."

Susan encouraged her to pursue dressage, but at first Donna didn't get it. "What was so exciting about riding around in circles?" she wondered. She didn't see the point.

But she was addicted to riding again, and very excited about the para-equestrian path. When she heard about a para-equestrian camp to be held in glorious San Juan Capistrano, California, she immediately booked herself a spot. There she met a group of other aspiring para-equestrians. Until then, Donna had been unsure about whether she wanted to just ride for pleasure, or become a serious competitor again. The event confirmed in her mind that she wanted to be competitive, and compete in dressage.

The feedback she got from the camp motivated her. Told she had "tons of raw talent, a great seat, and good, independent hands," she was hooked. She knew she had to go for it. Looking back now, though, she admits, "When they said I had raw talent, I had no idea how raw they meant."

Although the 2012 Olympics were approaching, and every serious competitor seems to aspire to the Olympics, Donna had no idea of the amount of work required. "Now," she says, "I know!"

At the time, Donna had an off-the-track Thoroughbred mare named Belle of the Ball that she was riding. She took Belle to a dressage show at Windy Hollow Hunt in Florida, New York, competing as a disabled rider in an able-bodied show. In the Introductory Level, she and the mare won all their classes.

However, the mare and Donna parted company far too often, as the mare couldn't tolerate Donna's imbalance. In addition, she was a "mareish" mare. After a bad fall put Donna in the hospital for two weeks in intensive care, Donna stopped riding her. Although she kept the mare, others at the barn began riding her.

Instead Donna began riding Kristi and Sue Niblo's horse, Otto. It was a perfect fit. Donna and the Niblos tease that Otto is short for "Autopilot." Otto is just the "Steady Eddie" that Donna needs, unperturbed by her changes in balance. "He is my world, he gave me my confidence back, he's so steady and sweet, such a tryer."

The match worked out so well that when Kristi went off to college (she plans on becoming a veterinarian), the Niblos, who had planned to lease Otto out, free leased him to Donna.

In June, Donna showed Otto at Training Level against able-bodied riders. They placed second out of 16 horses! In March, 2011, they traveled to California for a CDI. That didn't go too well, with scores running in the 50's. While other judges were more tactful, the Swedish judge told Donna, "You have to go home, and learn the art."

Donna did just that. Returning home, she went in search of a trainer. FEI rider and instructor Wes Dunham of Woodstock Stables in Millbrook, New York, was the result of her search. Wes, who trains Sue Niblo as well, is "the reason I'm a dressage rider," states Donna. "He makes Lendon Gray look easy. He's the toughest instructor. I've been an athlete all my life, but he really pushes me."

It was at this point that Donna realized what everyone

meant by "raw" talent. When she demonstrated to Wes what she thought was a good extended trot, he responded with, "Now you're finally showing me a trot." He wasn't referring to an *extended* trot, to Wes, it was a good *working* trot.

Now Wes couldn't be more proud of Donna. "She's been a real inspiration to my entire barn, myself included. She never complains. She gets out of her wheelchair, we help her on the horse, and she goes out and gives it her all.

Her determination is remarkable and her drive to compete at the top level is phenomenal."

Wes didn't have to change his training methods in order to work with Donna's physical challenges. "I still teach the basic concepts of dressage, but we use different tools to compensate." Since Donna doesn't have the use of her legs or seat, the horses she rides have been trained to respond, both forwards and sideways, to a whip on either side.

Donna isn't the only athlete in Wes' barn who stays fit. Wes insists that all his riders work out. "They're athletes; they have to train and be fit. You can't expect the horse to be an athlete and compete if the rider isn't an athlete as well."

Understanding the magnitude of her goal, Donna's daily routine begins before sunrise. Five days a week she is in the gym before beginning work at Putnam Independent Living Services. After work, she heads to the barn to train until after dark with Wes. Then she's homeward bound to review what she's learned, complete paperwork, and research and apply for funding opportunities to finance her quest.

Donna's initial resistance to dressage is long gone. At first, she didn't understand the beauty of it, and didn't think it was enough of a challenge. Still grieving over the rider she'd been, she finally started to understand that dressage is much more than making circles. Donna read Xenophon, and Alois Podjasky (at one time the director of the Spanish Riding School, and an Olympic medalist in dressage), and began to see the light. And the beauty. Dressage was about becoming one with your horse.

The turning point for Donna came when she competed at a dressage show at HITS in Saugerties, New York. A hunter/jumper show was taking place at the same time, so she wandered over to watch. She found it interesting, but, enamored now by dressage, she discovered she no longer missed jumping!

Donna's job at Putnam Independent Living Services enables her to give encouragement to other people with disabilities and their families. Donna coordinates a program that works with residents at nursing homes to enable them to transition back into the community. Although with all the budget cuts in the state it can be frustrating at times, "when it happens, there's no better feeling."

Her disability also stands her in good stead in her position. Seeing Donna, who looks quite disabled, come to their houses, work with them, and then leave to go ride her horses, gives people with disabilities and their families a pretty good idea that there are a lot of possibilities available to them.

Donna gets them thinking, and thinking out of the box!

Donna also enjoys doing demonstrations for 4-H groups, planting seeds, helping kids to understand not to judge someone's abilities by their appearance. She finds those demonstrations "very gratifying."

As well as Otto, Donna now has another superb mount. Wes lets her ride his eight-year-old mare Western Rose (Rosie) as a back up horse. Donna earned qualifying scores for the Para-Equestrian National Championships at Saugerties on *both* horses.

She went on to take the Championship on Otto, followed by only .3 of a point behind on Western Rose for the Reserve. Para-riders are classified according to the degree of their disability, and are required to have national and international classifications in order to compete. Donna competes in the Grade 1A division: for the most severely disabled.

Right after Nationals, Donna was one of eight riders selected to train with Robert Dover at USET Headquarters at Gladstone. She was thrilled! An opportunity to train with Robert Dover! How good does it get?!

Robert asked Donna how she and Rosie did at the National

Championships. Donna replied that they were Reserve Champions. When Robert asked her what the champion did better than she and Rosie had done, Donna replied, "She rode another horse." Donna then explained to Robert that she and Otto had taken the championship, and that Otto had "been steadier and we had displayed better harmony."

Donna "loves Rosie to death and I know we're going places. I just smile from ear to ear when I'm talking about her. We're starting to make a connection, to develop a bond."

One of the most amazing moments of Donna's life was when she got to represent the United States in Mexico City for the CPEDI*** (the Para-equestrian version of a CDI) in November, 2011. Donna rode a borrowed horse, Gecko, for the competition. At first she thought, "Oh great, I'm a quadriplegic, and I'm gonna catch ride. I was terrified."

Wes rode the horse first, and then gave her the lowdown: how much seat, whip, and half-halt the horse needed. Donna watched intently as he rode. Even after watching him, when she was getting a leg up on the horse, she was so nervous she thought she would be sick! But Gecko, a former show jumper and experienced para-equestrian horse, proved to be a star. In addition to winning Team Gold, Donna won the individual gold and freestyle in Grade 1A.

She says, "Wow! It was amazing. Such a sense of pride. To be up on the podium, with the American flag flying on the top pole and the national anthem playing. Sitting up there, thinking, 'I am so proud to be am American right now!'

There's an overwhelming pride and the satisfaction of representing your country and doing the best that you can. It was another moment when I wished time would stand still."

The following month she was off to a CPEDI*** in Melbourne, Australia. This time Donna experienced another dream. Her favorite dressage stallion was the legendary Donnerhall. In Melbourne Donna got the ride on Don Armani, a grandson of Donnerhall! As soon as she saw Don Armani, she thought she recognized his breeding, and her instinct proved correct. Don Armani was "just magnificent! Riding him the first time I felt omnipotent; he had *presence!* So this is what a dressage horse feels like, I thought."

For the first time in her life, Donna scored in the 70's. Wes, normally stone-faced and unemotional, saw the score, and came running over, pumping his fists in the air and yelling. Throwing his arms around her, he said, "You did it! You got your 70!"

Despite the fabulous results, Donna is taking nothing for granted. She has qualified for the Paralympic Selection Trials, which will take place in May at either the Kentucky Horse Park or Majestic Farms in Ohio. At that point the team for London will be selected.

Since Donna was financially unable to compete in Wellington in the winter of 2011, she lost her number one ranking. She hopes to compete at the CPEDI*** in Katy, Texas, in April, the last event before the Selection Trials, to give her a chance to compete and scope out the competition.

One of the hardest parts of the sport is the fundraising. Donna is excited that Marshall and Sterling Insurance recently came on board as her first major sponsor. She has a sponsorship page on her website and the local papers have helped spread the word. Donna sends letters to businesses to promote herself. She is so grateful, especially in this economy, for all the people who send her $10 or $20 to help her towards her goals.

A local 4-H club, "Whinnies and Neighs," which came to watch her ride, is holding a tag sale to raise money for her. Wes, who is "extremely proud to be part of this journey," doesn't charge her for lessons or coaching her at all of her shows. And a local public relations firm, Bang and Collins, has donated their services to helping her raise the needed money. In addition, the Niblos have been huge sponsors.

Just as it takes a village to raise a child, it takes one to send a para-athlete to the Paralympics. Donna counts herself very lucky. "I have so much talent to tap into. I am so fortunate to have my village. I always let people know how indebted I am to them. I am so lucky to have so many great people behind me."

She always keeps in mind Susan's words of wisdom. "Whatever the outcome, make sure you take the time to enjoy the journey." Although it's a struggle to live with MS, Donna would be reluctant to give it up. "My disability has allowed me to meet people and do things I would never have been able to do otherwise. I'm loving the journey!"

(If you'd like to help Donna reach her goal of competing at the London Paralympics, log on to (www.donnasdestiny.com) and go to the sponsorship page. Any amount will help move the journey forward.

⟶ HORSES fOR HEROES:
GIVING BACK TO VETERANS

There was little that Howard, a wheelchair bound veteran living in a residential care program, took an interest in. Howard, who had no use of his legs, and very limited use of his arms and hands, wasn't even interested in eating.

Life improved rapidly when Howard came to High Hopes Therapeutic Riding, Inc. in Old Lyme, Connecticut to take part in a new program, "Heroes for High Hopes." The first encouraging sign came when, after a short visit with Shetland pony Smokey, Howard came in for lunch—and dove right into his food!

High Hopes is accredited by NARHA (the national certification and education organization), which had started a new program, Horses for Heroes, providing nationwide support for America's wounded service personnel. Our veterans have risked their lives for their country; they have given us so much. NARHA wanted to give something back.

After witnessing what horses do for thousands of children and adults across the country with a variety of physical and mental limitations, NARHA decided to start a pilot program (in conjunction with Walter Reed Army Medical Center) to reach out to our veterans. Our war veterans, from World War II to Iraq and Afghanistan, suffer from a host of afflictions ranging from lost limbs to depression and anxiety.

The results of the pilot program, which included improved balance, posture, muscle strength and self-esteem, convinced NARHA to develop the program. The ability of horses to connect with people and promote healing makes them a perfect match for the veterans. Although many veterans are initially skeptical, once in the presence of a horse they quickly become fans of the program.

Heroes for High Hopes, which is provided with scholarship support, puts veterans and horses together in a therapeutic setting that brings out the best in everyone.

The improvement shown in Howard was not just in his appetite. Initially Howard sought out contact with Smokey himself, brushing and petting the pony whenever he could. But one day Smokey sought out Howard. While Howard was busy listening to the instructors, Smokey sauntered up next to Howard's motorized wheelchair and nudged the joystick, causing the chair to lurch forward. It was no accident. Smokey did it again, letting Howard know that he needed his attention!

Grooming Smokey and learning to drive Candy, another horse at High Hopes, (in a special carriage equipped to hold Howard's wheelchair) created a special bond with horses...a bond that changed Howard's life.

The veterans from the residential home all learned to work together with the horses, helping each other in a team-oriented approach. The weekly trip to High Hopes gave them something to look forward to, a new interest in their lives.

Another High Hopes student, Albert, says his depression lifted when he joined the High Hopes sessions. "I had never before experienced a horse,...but with the artful support of the staff, a person can touch, feel, communicate, direct and wonder about this magnificent messenger of the gods."

Chris, another program participant, says, "I have always liked horses but I had no idea that the therapeutic value of interacting with such an intelligent, graceful animal could be so great. I have grown particularly fond of a horse named Doc. His presence takes away all my anxiety. When I am working with Doc I feel a complete sense of peace and serenity."

A Baylor University study following veterans in the Georgetown, Texas, Horses for Heroes program showed improved mental health and decreased depression among the participants.

High Hopes has 21 horses of different sizes and abilities working in the program. The veterans each work with one specific horse in order to develop a bond. By not only riding, but caring for the horse they develop a trusting relationship with the animal.

Although the Heroes for High Hopes program began with Vietnam and World War II vets, recently they have been working with women who have done tours in Iraq.

Kathryn is a sergeant and combat veteran who served proudly in the United States Marine Corps from 2002-2007. She was stationed all over the U.S. and Japan, and deployed to Iraq. Since the end of her enlistment she has had an extremely difficult time with family relationships and friendships.

She says, "I have difficulty eating, sleeping, and functioning without a high level of anxiety."

Her experience with Heroes for High Hopes has been life changing. Kathryn had always loved horses and looked into therapeutic riding. Her first thought was to call High Hopes to get information on volunteering. But, "When I called I asked if they have any programs for Veterans and it turned out that they were looking for Vet participants, I signed up that same week and applied for the scholarship.

Every Friday for about a month now, I have enjoyed working with staff at High Hopes and Leila (my horse). The time that I have spent there has had a tremendous impact on helping me with my anxiety. When I am with Leila nothing else seems to matter; no matter what intrusive thoughts I have had over the week they all seem to disappear for that hour. The way Leila responds to me and how we work together can only be described as spiritual. I have been truly blessed to have the opportunity to work with Leila and the wonderful individuals at High Hopes. I continue to practice the coping skills that I have learned and apply them to my daily life. I will be forever grateful for the kindness they have shown me and all the support they provided. I will carry this experience in my heart forever."

NARHA, which boasts over 700 member centers and serves more than 36,000 participants nationwide, is putting a great deal of effort into developing the Horses for Heroes programs across the country. At the Virginia facility, able bodied participants in the program are trained to help others as they come in. The horses used are the "Caisson Platoon" horses, the horses that escort service members killed in action (and those ranked sergeant major and above at the time of their death) to their final resting place at Arlington National Cemetery. This is the platoon whose horses accompanied the funerals of John Kennedy, Lyndon Johnson and General Douglas MacArthur and included the famous Black Jack.

Horses for Heroes is a program that can help veterans find peace and joy in their lives. Veterans interested in the program can contact their local NARHA facility for more information.

Neville Bardos and Boyd Martin
Photo: Diana De Rosa

Reckless with Joe Latham
from the Nancy Latham Parkin collection.

Photo credits: Lindsay Y McCall for USPEA

Donna Ponessa with Rosie and Otto

Photo credit: Carola Lott

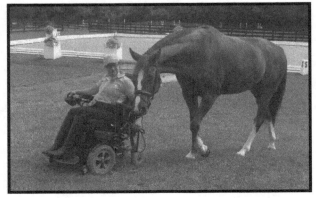

ROCK STARS

⟿ fINDING SKYE

Like so many little girls, *Ice Road Trucker* Lisa Kelly loved horses, and loved to collect every model horse she could get her hands on. Breyers™, My Little Pony™, any horses Lisa found, she had to have.

Lisa started riding in Sterling, Alaska, where her mother kept a few horses. Pepper, the most stubborn, meanest pony there, was her first mount. Displaying the strong will to learn and overcome obstacles that serves her in good stead driving trucks on the world's most dangerous roads, Lisa wouldn't give up. "We were both stubborn, so it worked out. I was more stubborn, so I won." Lisa had to learn to ride Pepper before she was allowed to get a horse of her own.

After managing to outwit the willful Pepper, she was rewarded with her first horse, Poncho, a Palomino that she had for nearly 20 years. The Arab/Quarter Horse cross was "the best horse I ever had. I had so much fun with him! As a teenager I could just get out of the house and disappear into the woods." Lisa rode Western, and loved exploring Alaska's endless trails. But when Poncho reached his 30's, Lisa knew he wouldn't be around too much longer. It was time to get another horse.

Wanting a spotted horse, she began scouring ads in the local newspaper. Lisa came across a Tennessee Walker filly, advertised as spotted. When she made arrangements to go see the horse, she found the color disappointing. Skye, a weanling black Tennessee Walker, had splashes of white, but not as much color as Lisa had hoped.

Lisa may have been disappointed in the color, but Skye knew from the start that she would be going to a new home with

Lisa. Following her around like a puppy, practically in Lisa's pocket, Skye instantly won her heart.

"She was such a sweetheart. I would have been stupid not to buy her; she was just so sweet," Lisa recalls. It would be years before she could ride Skye, but that didn't matter. Lisa was smitten. Skye came home to live with Poncho at Lisa's mom's house. For a while, although Lisa owned two horses, she couldn't ride either one of them. Poncho was too old; Skye too young.

Keeping horses in Alaska is an entirely different matter from keeping them in the lower 48. It's extremely pricey, as hay can be hard to come by and prohibitively expensive. Horses are allowed to grow heavy coats to protect them from the acute cold. Although they do have barns, the horses live out for the most part because going in and out all the time would be harder on them with the variance in temperature.

As Skye began to grow, Lisa didn't get to spend too much time with her. Pursuing her new career in trucking, Lisa had moved four hours away from where Skye lived. Between learning her new job, working a lot of hours, and moving to where the work was, Lisa was separated from Skye for long periods of time.

Lisa's job is not for the faint of heart. Lisa drives the James W. Dalton Highway, better known as "the haul road," a 414 mile route running from north of Fairbanks to Prudhoe Bay, Alaska. The road was built to support the Trans-Alaska Pipeline System, and parallels it.

The road didn't achieve its standing as one of the world's most dangerous roads without reason. Trucks are literally driving on ice. Seventy miles north of Fairbanks the pavement ends, and a 2" layer of ice becomes the new road surface. Big rigs require a smooth surface, and no other material can stand up under these extreme weather conditions. The trade-off is that often drivers find themselves hauling immense loads on a surface as slick as a skating rink.

Drivers face grades as steep as 12 percent on this slippery road bed, and must run a gauntlet of challenges which include "the taps" (a series of steep hills and sharp curves), the high, narrow, and glassy Yukon River Bridge, "the roller coaster" which features nearly vertical drops, Atigun Pass (the highest point on the route at a height of 4700', and subject to avalanches), and the Shelf. The route's steep grades, sharp corners, and icy roadbed are not the only challenges. A truck that breaks down can mean death for the driver in temperatures that can drop to 60 below. (The lowest recorded temperature in Prudhoe Bay, one of the coldest places on earth, was an astounding -82 degrees F). Zero visibility due to "a blow," or whiteout, can cause drivers to drive right off the road or into an oncoming truck.

George Spears, a war veteran who drove the haul road for 30 years, calls it "the closest thing to combat I could find." In fact, the drivers are paid so well for traversing this route that they earn the equivalent of combat pay. Driving on ice roads is clearly a job for those who like to live life on the edge.

Lisa began her career on the ice road as one of only three women out of 200 drivers. Lisa doesn't drive the road because she has to. She became a truck driver "because I wanted to." She drives the haul road "because I want to."

Her first experience on the Dalton was in the summer, and it seemed like "just another road." After Lisa started driving it in winter she realized "The more you see of what can happen, the more you understand just how dangerous it is."

Although she recognizes those dangers, she says, "It's just something you kind of learn and get accustomed to."

Lisa has grown up driving on ice, so her usual driving style worked perfectly for her job. "I drive slowly and carefully, no sudden accelerations, no sudden stops. I pretend there's an egg under my pedal and try not to break it: it's all controlled and careful and easy. I approach stop signs so slowly I'm basically stopped by the time I get there."

In addition to her driving style, gears are crucially important to driving the ice roads. The right gear makes all the difference between success or failure on the steep hills. Drivers also utilize a jake brake, an engine braking mechanism which slows the truck without burning out the brakes on trucks and trailers, especially on steep downhill runs.

Lisa enjoys doing "heavy hauls": driving the largest, heaviest, most unwieldy loads. In order to stay on, and negotiate the road with those loads, she says, "You have to trust the guy in front of you. You follow him, stay hooked up with him, and trust him."

Lisa is known for her drive, and desire to continually challenge herself. She says, "It's important to know yourself, and it takes a long time to learn it. My love of challenges has just been developing all along."

One of the challenges Lisa took on recently was driving the "death" roads of Bolivia and Peru. Although she'd checked them out on YouTube before agreeing to drive them, the actual in-person view was far more frightening. And it wasn't only the roads. The trucks were in terrible shape, with problems involving brake failure and loss of steering.

Lisa thought over the commitment that she had made, and considered whether it was worth it. Under the circumstances, it would have been "just stupid to continue. I thought about giving up and going home. But I decided I would do it, if I could do it under my terms." Lisa would only drive if the truck was fixed to her specifications. The truck was fixed, and Lisa went on to safely, and successfully, complete her assignment.

She's not sure where she gets her drive from, but her father likely played a role in it. "He just picked himself up and moved to Alaska, and learned to fly an airplane." Sounds a lot like the Lisa we know and love.

As Lisa spent more and more time on the road, perfecting her driving skills and taking on more, and more challenging, loads, her relationship with Skye remained strong. Every time Lisa came home, Skye ran to greet her, welcoming her joyfully.

That all changed one day when Lisa was filming in Prudhoe Bay. She heard shocking news. Through a series of circumstances, Skye was no longer at her mother's farm. "Where was she? Was she all right? Was she being cared for?" Devastated and worried sick, Lisa determined that she would track her down and find her.

It didn't prove to be easy. For nearly a year, Lisa attempted to locate her horse, "chasing her around the country." She knew that she and Skye shared a special bond, and Lisa's stubbornness served her well. She would not give up until she located her horse.

She did, at least, have Rocky, a miniature horse (and yes, Rocky has spots). Living in a rented home, Lisa couldn't keep a full size horse with her. In order to have a horse in her life, she got a miniature. The miniature, however, often seems to think he's a big dog.

When Lisa returns from life on the road, Rocky invites himself into the house, gives her hugs, and shares snacks like peanut butter with her. He and Lisa's Sphynx cat, Tanzi, enjoy hanging out together, and Rocky enjoys watching movies with Lisa and her husband Travis.

Rocky rides in the back of the pickup truck, sometimes sticking his head into the front seat as though wondering why he isn't in front like the other passengers. He and Lisa hike together, with Rocky carrying his own backpack. Lisa hoped Rocky might prove to be a good jogging partner, but that dream ended when Lisa discovered Rocky's plans didn't mesh with hers. Dragging a stubborn pony behind her while she jogged was more work than Lisa intended.

Rocky enjoys accompanying Lisa and Travis to motocross events. (Driving trucks on ice roads is not Lisa's only extreme occupation: she was state motocross champion, and skydives frequently with Travis.)

Lisa acquired Rocky through a fan who breeds minis. Although the man gave her Rocky, initially Lisa couldn't figure out how to get the horse up to Alaska. Ground transportation proved exorbitantly expensive. Luckily, when Lisa looked into flights, she discovered they were quite affordable, so Rocky took a plane to his new home in Alaska.

A baby when he arrived, Rocky only reached Lisa's knee. He since has learned many tricks, including bowing, fetching, shaking hands, and pulling a cart. However adorable he is, he's also "a little pain in the butt; he bites and kicks."

Rocky loves being in the limelight: in fact he steals it most of the time. He's been on CNN, has his own "Rocky's Nation" on Lisa's website, and has his own fan page.

Great with kids, Rocky happily puts up with them crawling all over him. When one of Lisa's friend's kids was in the hospital, Lisa took Rocky to visit the child to cheer him up. Although they couldn't bring Rocky into the hospital, they could bring the child out to Rocky. He lay down in the grass, and Rocky lay down in the grass right next to him. Rocky has proven himself so good at understanding the needs of children that Lisa is having him certified as a therapy horse.

Rocky has no idea he's a miniature: he sees himself as a big horse. He's also "a total camera hog, he sticks his nose right in the camera. You can't take a photo without him in it!" Rocky has play dates with other miniatures in the area, and has dressed up as an angel, and a unicorn, among other costumes for holidays.

Although Lisa loves Rocky, he can't replace a full-size horse in her life. Lisa was determined to find Skye. Her philosophy is, "If you want something, don't sit there and wait for it. Go get it!" She kept up her search. In time a rumor reached Lisa that a fellow motocross racer was dating the woman who had Skye. At a motocross track in Anchorage, Lisa ran into them.

"I heard a rumor that you have my horse," Lisa said to the woman.

"I do have your horse."

Lisa instantly lost control of her emotions. "Oh my gosh, I bawled like a baby!" she recalls. She told the woman, "I have to come see her! I'll be down this weekend." Lisa's emotions were mixed: from the joy of finding her horse at last, to the sadness over their separation and the anger at what had caused it.

That weekend she raced to the woman's home to see her horse. Hearing Lisa's voice, Skye came tearing right over to her. She had been missing Lisa as much as Lisa missed her.

Unfortunately it was only a temporary reunion, for despite all of Lisa's work to track her down, getting Skye back wouldn't be easy. She *was* going to get her back; she would find a way. She just had to figure out how.

Lisa wasn't sure where she would keep Skye. She didn't think she would be allowed to keep Skye at home as there were no facilities on the land for keeping her there. Still, there was space.

Lisa talked to her landlord. Could they build a place to keep Skye? To her amazement he agreed. Skye could come and live there.

"*Really!* I can bring my horse!" Lisa exclaimed joyfully. All the pain and frustration was disappearing. Lisa knew Skye would come home to live with her. Now all she needed to do was earn the money to put in the fencing and barn, plus lay in a good supply of hay, not a cheap commodity in Alaska.

Meanwhile, Skye was sold back to Roberta, the woman who had bred her, with Roberta promising to keep her for Lisa. It was all right; Lisa now knew where Skye was, and that she was safe and in a good home.

Lisa knew she would have to drive as many loads as she could on the demanding ice roads to bring Skye home.

One day while she was in Fairbanks, Lisa discovered a Schleich™ horse model she didn't have, a black horse. She purchased it to add to her collection. Once she returned to her truck, she showed it to her cameraman. He inquired if Lisa had bought it as a prompt, to encourage her to take extra loads to earn Skye back. Although it hadn't been Lisa's intention, it worked. Whenever Lisa needed to focus on her goal, she picked up the black horse and was reminded of Skye waiting for her. "It gave me something to focus on. You want to take more loads. You add up all the expenses and it motivates you to keep going. I had the money to buy her, but not feed her and keep her."

Skye, meanwhile, had been bred, and was now a mother herself. Even when the preparations for her living quarters were finished, Lisa had to put off their reunion until Skye's baby was old enough to be weaned.

Eventually, all the time, all the extra loads, paid off. Skye came home. "The day I bought her was such a good feeling. She's *mine*, and she's never going anywhere again."

After weeks on the ice road, Lisa can't wait to come home to see Skye and Rocky. She rides Skye right out of her backyard on to the trails, with Rocky accompanying them. (Rocky comes in handy, when Lisa couldn't find any way to get up on Skye bareback, Rocky was right there, so...she used him as a mounting block.)

If Lisa can't decide whether to ride, or do errands, no worries. She jumps on Skye and heads into town where she first stops at the local coffee shop, riding up to the take-out window to get her coffee to go. She did discover a discrepancy when she rode up to the window and found that although they kept treats for dogs that went through the drive-in window, there were none for horses. Lisa plans to correct this omission by donating some horse treats so that Skye, and her friends' horses, can get their own rewards when going through.

Now that she has her coffee, she's ready to do her chores on horseback. It may take her "eight hours, but it's so much fun!"

The horses are not Lisa's only pets. She has two cats, a Ragdoll named Kitty who was rescued from the pound and was their first animal, and Tanzi. (Lisa had always wanted a Sphynx.) Lisa keeps it to two cats because she doesn't want people "to see me as a crazy cat lady!" She also has a dog acquired on her latest shoot in the Andes of Peru. The dog she rescued in *Most Dangerous Roads* in the Himalayas was adopted by the film's producer. (You can read his story, available on Lisa's website, www.thelisakelly.com).

Skye has been back with Lisa for over a year now, and their bond continues to grow. Lisa rides with an Australian stock saddle (ever since she was really little, says Lisa, "I wanted all the Australian gear, now I've got it!"), or an endurance saddle when she's not riding bareback. She's also been known to snowboard behind a horse. Trying to increase her knowledge about horses, Lisa took Skye to a Parelli clinic, where Skye "did everything I asked, she was awesome!"

Lisa is ecstatic to have Skye back in her life. "She's a blast; I've had so much fun on her and she's turned out to be the nicest little riding horse ever. She's so easy to teach! I take her jogging with me. There's so much we can learn together, do together, we have so much fun together! We spend hours with each other. I'll never sell her in my entire life. I'm living my dreams with her: either on top of her, or next to her."

~⁀⁀ PADRÉ

He is the "ultimate underdog." When the stunning stallion with his bright dun coat and waves of silky black tresses was named Reserve Champion Stallion at Dressage at Devon in 2010, he confounded onlookers curious about his origins. German riding pony? Lusitano? Andalusian? Welsh cob? Nobody guessed correctly.

Padré is an American Mustang.

And yes, it was the first time in history that a Mustang qualified for, and competed at, Devon.

Patti Gruber, a dressage trainer from Illinois, wanted a new dressage partner, a horse that could be competitive at the upper levels. She was thinking along the lines of an Art Deco pinto warmblood.

Patti always brought her horses to the International Equine Podiatry Center in Versailles, Kentucky to be looked at by veterinarian Dr. Rick Redden. Dr. Redden owned the center's Mustangs and Patti would always joke, "If you ever want to see what one of these horses can do, let me know."

Dr. Redden had been studying the relationship of genetics in over-bred domestic breeds. His focus was to determine if leg problems could be eliminated by breeding domestic mares with his genetically pure Mustang stallion Padré. Padré came from the Palomino Valley herd outside Reno, Nevada, and had been captured as a yearling.

Dr. Redden often spoke of the great personality and quiet nature of the horse, traits the stallion always passed on to his offspring. Patti had watched Padré grow from a gawky two-year-old to a beautiful seven-year-old. She'd always admired his natural ability and undeniable presence, along with his sweet temperament.

One day Dr. Redden took her up on her offer. Would she like Padré? The timing couldn't have been worse. Patti had just gotten divorced. She had cats, dogs, and other horses. The Art Deco baby remained in her head. This wasn't what she had thought about for her dressage partner. But there was no turning down this magnificent horse.

Padré was sent to a Western trainer, Nathan Stephens, for a 30 day introduction to life in a stable complete with a regular work schedule instead of the life of leisure he had known.

Nathan had worked with many Mustangs before and understood their difference from domestic breeds. Since Padré and Nathan were seven hours from where Patti lived, many hours were spent that month on the phone discussing how well Padré was adapting to his new working life, and his particular nuances.

Nathan repeatedly told Patti that to be successful with Padré she had to earn his trust, and respect him. After the 30 days were up Patti traveled to Nathan's farm to take her horse home. She rode Padré for the first time in a round pen. As they started off Patti found herself amazed by the amount of power Padré had for a 15.1 hand horse. With each gait his power increased and she began to realize his true athletic ability.

The next morning, Padré and Patti left for Wayfarer Farm in Wauconda, Illinois where Patti trains and teaches, to begin bonding and building trust with one another.

After riding him only three times their first week at home Patti took Padre to a clinic with a well-respected German trainer, Andre Heufler. Patti didn't mention that Padré was a Mustang, as she wanted Andre to judge and work with them based on Padré's ability, not his breed. At the end of the weekend when she revealed Padré's origins to Andre, he was stunned. He was also very impressed with the stallion's ability, and recommended that Patti enter him in a schooling show at his barn, Sunflower Farm in Bristol, Wisconsin, in three weeks.

Patti thought it was too soon to compete. Andre thought

that Padré had enough natural talent to compete in dressage and get good scores despite his extremely limited training.

Andre was right. Padré did better than Patti could ever have imagined. Entering two classes, Green as Grass 1 Horse and Green as Grass 4 Horse, they won both their tests, with scores of 67.65% and 64.5 % respectively. After they finished their rides, judge Joan Pecora called them over to satisfy her curiosity about Padré's breeding, background, and training. Naturally she was surprised to find out that he was a Mustang and that he had only been in dressage training for three weeks! She told Patti that Padré had a good future in dressage, and a great natural rhythm. She encouraged them to continue, and said she would look forward to seeing them in the future. Padré finished the day with the High Point award for the division!

"We did better than I could have ever imagined for his first show," says Patti.

Andre, who continues to train Patti and Padré (currently working at Third/Fourth Level), trained in Germany with Conrad Schumacher, and then moved to this country to work for Temple Farms with their Lippizan stallions. His experience with stallions has given him great insight into working with Padré.

Patti and Padré have participated in several clinics and with each clinic Padré has shown the clinicians his intelligence, natural ability, bold movements and quiet disposition. When the pair worked with Steffen Peters during the 2010 Midwest Horse Fair in Wisconsin, Steffen paid them a great compliment. He told Patti that he could "see something special" in them.

Although Padré is still a stallion, Patti turns him out with six geldings without a problem. He is a perfect gentleman both while out on trails and working in the arena with mares that are in heat.

Padré was named an ambassador for the Bureau of Land Management Wild Horse and Burro Program, and represents the program at Equine Affaire in Columbus, Ohio. With thousands or people coming by and stopping to see him, Padré was a rock.

It was while at Equine Affaire that Patti realized, "There

are so many people who don't realize there are still mustangs in the wild, and that they are naturally gifted. A lot of people think Mustangs are crass and rough and you can't do anything with them. Padré proves them wrong."

She does caution potential owners. "Mustangs differ depending on what herd management area they are from, as they are built for their particular environment. They vary in height, color and build. People must keep in mind that they are wild and are guided in life by instinct. Mustangs view their people and other horses as part of their herd. They are not a horse for everyone. To work with them successfully one must be patient and kind, and understand that the only way to develop a successful partnership is by building trust and listening to them."

Patti doesn't limit Padré to strictly dressage. They tried their hand at halter classes at American Buckskin Registry Association shows, where Padré took Reserve Champion stallion their first time out. They've had very good placings in hunter under saddle classes. "There's nothing he can't go and do. People, whether it's judges or spectators, are fascinated and don't really know what to do with him, since he looks and moves a little differently from horses he competes against. He challenges people's perceptions."

When a friend recommended Patti try in-hand classes at dressage sport horse breeding competitions, Patti jumped right in. In their first try they placed third in the 4-year-old and older stallion class, scoring a 75. Patti didn't think much about it. She had no idea how good or bad the score might be. Next they competed in the Great American Insurance Group/United States Dressage Federation Breeders' Championship Regional Finals, taking home the blue in the 4-year-old and older stallions and the reserve Grand Championship.

Working with Padré has presented Patti with both challenges and victories. "I'm learning how to read him; he really tells me when I'm doing something wrong." Patti spends a lot of time playing with him, working on body language. "He has a wonderful attitude; he doesn't kick or bite. He's *so* smart I have to be careful how I teach him because if I teach him wrong; I have to go back and re-teach him. He learns the first time you teach him anything."

She can't believe how much she has learned about working with all the horses she has in training simply by listening to Padré. "I am a better trainer," she says, "because of him."

Padré is not shy about expressing an opinion. If Patti nags him too much with her spurs, he picks up a back foot on the side. He kicks at her foot to let her know that he got the point. When he has had enough he will plant his feet, turn his head to look at Patti and snort as though saying, "I have had enough and if you ask me one more time I am going to have to give you a non-playful buck." Then they take a deep breath and move on to something else.

Padré has quite a sense of humor and loves to make Patti laugh. With his long hair and regal mentality, he will not go out of the barn in the rain. He peeks out the door, but refuses to go outside and get wet. He enjoys breakfast (and dinner) in bed. If his grain is served in his ground feed pan while he is in the middle of a nap he will remain lying down as he eats. Although he loves carrots and apples, he has also acquired a taste for french fries, marshmallow peeps, jelly beans, peaches, bananas and ice cream. He enjoys his warm, comfy blankets in the winter and a cooling, sudsy bath in the summer. His attitude is "I am the coolest thing on four legs!"

His connection with Patti is outstanding and unmistakable, whether he is giving her everything he's got at a show, or giving her kisses under the mistletoe in his stall.

Patti spends hours caring for his hair. She says, "My own hair is short now because I spend so much time taking care of his!"

Patti wasn't planning to go to Devon. In fact she thought it was way out of their reach. But she discovered that the in-hand score of 75 that they had achieved qualified her for Dressage at Devon. Her first thought was "Panic! How do I get there? How do I get my Mustang half way across the country?"

Fundraising provided the money for the trip, and Patti was thrilled with the tremendous community support for Padré.

At Devon Patti found herself in awe of what was happening. "Just knowing the caliber of horses, and I'm standing among them in a championship class with my little wild stallion without the genetic gifts and generations of selective breeding that these horses have—that was my proudest moment."

The little wild stallion won the in-hand 4-year-old and older stallions class and won lots of praise from the judges as well. Janine Malone said "This horse showed very consistent and clear rhythm at the walk and trot, and in particular the walk was active and ground-covering."

Hilda Gurney said "This stallion was by far the most correct in his class. Mother Nature did a nice job producing a nice-moving and very well-mannered mustang."

"Can you see the mascara running down my face?" says Patti, referring to the photo of she and Padré winning the class. "This has exceeded my wildest dreams. I've never been to Devon before, and it felt so far out of the realm of possibility. But everyone here has been so welcoming, the judges so kind, the officials so generous and helpful. I wish every show could be like this; I could not have asked for a better experience."

Patti is so proud of her horse. "He's raising awareness, inspiring people." She gets numerous emails from people who are inspired to try more things with their own horses, whether Mustangs or other breeds. Padré gives a great deal of hope to people.

Patti recently received a note from Nathan Stephens on Padré's Facebook page. "Hey Patti," he wrote, "I had Padré and broke him for Doc. It looks like he's doing well. I always knew he was a very special horse. To this day, he is still the nicest horse I ever swung my leg across!"

In September, 2011, at the Great American Insurance Group/USDF North Central Series Division Finals Padre' was named Grand Champion Stallion receiving his highest score ever in hand, 76.125 %. The judges' comments included: strongly built, presence, active, correct rhythm, uses body well, good reach and swing through back, well behaved, cooperative and willing with promise and potential. The Reserve Grand Champion horse was owned by the USDF Breeder of the Year and Padré was 4% ahead of him!

The show was held at Silverwood Farm in Camp Lake, Wisconsin. Although Patti "didn't think it could get any better than Devon, one Grand Championship ribbon, one Grand Championship cooler, and a plaque later, I think this definitely feels as good as Devon last year."

On the way home, Patti spoke to her trainer, who had suggested they compete in in-hand classes. Patti said she'd had a talk with Padré's before the class and explained how important this was since the only horse who had beaten them this season was in the class.

The trainer replied that Padré is a perfect mix of being serious in his work but a ham and a half when people are watching. Shortening it up, they decided that Padré is a Serious Ham.

"He is," Patti says, "such a good boy and makes my dreams come true. I could not have imagined four years ago when I got him that all this would have happened."

Patti and Padré have taken a journey no one ever would have thought possible. Patti took a wild horse, a horse few people would have believed in, and showed the world what he could do. She says, "Padré is the most amazing dressage partner I could have asked for. His presence, natural athletic ability and personality are phenomenal. I am lucky to have many horses to train but the best part of each day is when I work with Padré."

⟶ GUNNER'S SPECIAL NITE

G unner's Special Nite has had many very special nights, but one in 2010 was particularly memorable, in fact historic. At the United States Equestrian Federation's annual convention, "Bailey," a double-registered American Quarter Horse/American Paint Horse, became the first western horse to win USEF's Horse of the Year title. Bailey's trainer and rider, Tom Mc-Cutcheon, wasn't left in his wake, becoming the first reiner to earn the USEF Equestrian of the Year title. Tom and Bailey were individual and team gold medalists in the 2010 World Equestrian Games, while Tom is a National Reining Horse Association Million Dollar Rider.

Bailey is as close to perfect as a reining horse can get. Owned by Sarah Willeman, he is the kind of horse that make onlookers take one look and think, "I've got to take up reining. It looks like so much fun!"

Tom and Sarah first spotted Bailey at the National Reining Horse Association's Futurity, when Marcy ver Meer was showing him. Bailey was second in the three-year-old event. "It was such a memorable experience," says Sarah. "It was what reining should be."

Tom knew that Sarah was looking for a top breeding stallion, as well as a horse he could compete with at the World Equestrian Games. Tom and Sarah felt that with his athleticism and great mind, Bailey could be a top contender at the WEG. When the opportunity to purchase him came up, Tom found out about it, and they closed the deal.

Tom says, "He already had an accomplished show career; he was always a great show horse. Some horses just have that extra something, the ring presence, the look. To win at the top they have to have everything. They can't have any weak maneuvers. He was just the most complete horse I've ever seen. It was a no-brainer to go after him."

Bailey is by Tim McQuay's stallion Colonels Smoking Gun, one of the hottest sires in the world, out of Mifs Doll, a granddaughter of Smart Little Lena. Tom is Tim McQuay's son-in-law, married to Tim's daughter Mandy. Truly all in the family.

In evaluating Bailey to buy, Tom says, "Besides his looks and talent, a big part of it was his breeding. We had a lot of confidence in it. The breeding is what's under the hood; you can always fall back on it. It gave us a big comfort level in buying him."

The amazing relationship between Tom and Bailey didn't happen instantaneously. "I knew we would get along eventually, but it took a little while for the chemistry to develop. We had some things to work out, some stuff to figure out about each other." Tom figures it "took about 60 days for us to start firing on all cylinders. Even at the qualifiers we weren't quite there. But shortly thereafter we clicked."

Once they clicked, they *really* clicked. Sarah says, "It's one of those great partnerships. Tom couldn't have done a better job with him." Bailey, she says, "has so much heart and he tries so hard. We appreciate him so much."

Bailey made everyone's dreams come true when he not only qualified and competed at the WEG, but also won double gold with Tom, the only horse and rider to do so. Tom has been on all three WEG teams including Jerez, Spain in 2002, and Aachen, Germany in 2006, but having it here in the United States made it an entirely different affair. "I knew what to expect since I'd been there. I knew how to prepare the horses. In Spain we were just there to win, and that was all. But the crowds here, the fanfare, it was more than any of us expected. This time the focus was on winning too, but it was also on the experience. I had my wife and kids there and it made it really special."

Bailey, Tom says, is "real gritty. When he knows it's time to horse show, he puts on his helmet and tightens his chin strap and goes for it. He's just so great minded."

The team in Kentucky was a dream team, composed of Tom, his father-in-law Tim McQuay, Shawn Flarida, and Craig Schmersal. Tom says, "I don't know that we'll ever get the opportunity to put together a team like that again. In 20 or 30 years, I'll look back and say that I remember that team." And being on the same team as his father-in-law "made it extra special."

The winning run he made with Bailey for the individual medals was "just about perfect, as good as one can be."

Sarah says, "I practically fell out of my chair in the skybox when I saw the run. It was a good thing there were people in the box to keep me from falling out! It was one of those magical performances; they were both as on it as they could be. It was the best run I've ever seen!"

The judges agreed, scoring Bailey with a whopping 228.

Sarah says that Bailey "rose to the occasion and then some. With all his heart and athleticism he found a whole new level in himself."

After the WEG, Bailey retired to the breeding shed. Tom explains, "That's the biggest event in the history of reining, so there was just nowhere to go from there."

As the only horse who'd brought home double gold from Kentucky, Sarah and Tom knew he had a shot at the Horse of the Year title. Sarah says "I had my hopes up because what he'd done was so extraordinary. I kind of had a feeling."

Waiting for the results was nerve wracking. Tom says, "When David started getting the card out, and building the anticipation, I was super nervous." That quickly turned into "very excited" when he learned that Bailey had won. It was followed by his own win as Equestrian of the Year. "To win both was a big deal. I was actually there to experience it. When you're up there and you see all the people who had won it (Equestrian of the Year) before...

there are so many great horsemen on it. So it's pretty cool!"

Sarah "couldn't be happier that Tom is the one to achieve all this with a horse of mine."

Tom is quick to credit Sarah. "Sarah was a huge part of the whole thing. She was right on board and has been an amazing owner right from the start. Without her, none of it would have happened."

Bailey won close to a quarter of a million dollars during his competitive career. He's now "living the life, being a breeding stallion." And he knows he's the *king* of the barn.

Sarah says, "We try not to spoil him *too* much. He's done so much for us already." She spends time visiting with him, hanging out with him. Sarah makes sure that he knows just how much she and Tom appreciate him.

Bailey is now one of the most popular studs in the country. His first crop are yearlings now and Tom says, "He's really stamped them. We're really excited about them. He's being bred to the absolute best mares in the country. A lot of really big name trainers have them so this crop will get a lot of the right opportunities."

In an acceptance speech to the USEF convention when Bailey won Horse of the Year, Sarah summed it up. "I think this is the most exciting moment ever as a horse owner. It seems surreal...we haven't even had him for a year...We knew he was a phenomenal horse, and of course Tom has all the experience and expertise to achieve anything. But when you see a horse and rider click like that and just achieve something beyond what you ever could have imagined it's just amazing...I was thrilled just to see him on the U.S. team, and to see him contribute to the team's win at the WEG. But then his run with Tom in the individual final was really the best reining run that I've ever seen. It was one of those rare moments of greatness in sport."

⤳ FOR THE MOMENT

"**I** didn't make him a star, and he didn't make me a star. We helped each other to the top" says Lisa Jacquin about "For the Moment," a Thoroughbred jumper with whom she earned a Silver Medal in the Seoul Olympics. "Instead of training by the book, intuition, teamwork, and trust are what brought about our success."

Twenty-year-old Lisa was working for Leslie Burr at Fairfield County Hunt Club, riding some horses and getting some young riders started in their lessons when an as yet unnamed eight-year-old Thoroughbred was brought over so Leslie could have a look at him. Lisa didn't pay much attention. "He was just a horse, kind of skinny and scrawny and half wild." The 16.1 hand gelding had never been shown, or even jumped: he was a very green prospect.

Leslie (and Lisa) loved Thoroughbreds. The gelding had been purchased for $5000 from a claiming race. Although he was introduced to them as a potential children's hunter, he was "very racetracky. He didn't want to comply; he had his own ideas. And he only knew one speed."

Leslie had no problem seeing what was underneath Fred's (as he came to be called) rough exterior. The horse could jump, and she could tell there was quality there. He didn't jump like a hunter, with his high, stiff head carriage. He hung his legs. But he jumped high and clean.

When his owner brought him back a second time, Lisa rode him while Leslie watched. Leslie loved the horse, saying he had a lot of spring and power behind.

Lisa had just emerged from a very successful junior career and was taking her first professional steps. She was looking for a young jumper prospect, and Leslie suggested she purchase Fred as a project. If he didn't cut it as a top jumper, she could school him and resell him in order to purchase a more expensive horse.

Christmas was only a few weeks away, and Lisa was focused on being home with her family for the holidays. She left Connecticut without even thinking about Fred.

She had only been in Arizona for a few days when she was surprised by a phone call from Leslie. Leslie, along with Fairfield County Hunt Club's owner, Bruce Burr, had continued jumping Fred higher (up to four feet), as well as taking him over some combinations. The horse just kept improving. Leslie encouraged Lisa to buy him.

Lisa finally agreed, although it was due more to Leslie's enthusiasm than a strong desire on her part. Once she'd sent the check off in the mail, however, her feelings shifted. She now owned her very first horse! Hurrying back to Fairfield to start her relationship with him, she was greeted with a rump and pinned back ears. He wouldn't even eat the carrot she offered him.

Since Lisa had no idea if she would keep Fred, and he was quite possibly a temporary mount, he earned the name "For the Moment."

Lisa continued riding Leslie's jumpers while she became acquainted with Fred. The horse was a volatile mixture of power and bravery with a large dash of fear thrown in. He would jump just about anything if he was comfortable (often with an unsettling motion akin to a pogo stick) but if something unnerved him, he would shut right down. And he had a long list of things that upset him.

Lisa's background, training as a junior with Kaye Love back in Arizona, served her in good stead. She'd had the opportunity to ride really nice horses, and always had Kaye's full support. From Kaye she learned to be quiet with her hands and body, skills that proved crucial with Fred. She'd been lucky enough as well to ride with George Morris, Joe Fargis, and Conrad Holmfeld, always on quality horses. All of this sterling background came into play as Lisa brought Fred along.

Tense and nervous, Fred often took off with Lisa. He would

not be rated between fences; he wouldn't turn, stop, or swap leads. If Lisa tried to use her hands to rate or stop him, he would just stick his head in the air and keep going.

Standing martingales were useless. As soon as Fred felt the pressure, he went straight up. He broke three the first day. Stronger bits also sent his head straight in the air.

Lisa gave up on tack experimentation and spent more time doing flatwork.

Although Fred was always a very careful horse, he was very difficult for the first two years. He was Lisa's first "project" and "he taught me a lot. I taught him a lot. We were together from scratch."

Lisa took care of Fred herself, giving him a chance to bond with her and learn to trust her. She gave him every possible chance to be the best that he could be. She never rushed him, understanding that he could have been ruined as a young horse if he had been pushed too much. Pushing Fred would have fried his sensitive mind.

Leslie believes in letting a horse go the way that suits it the best, so she wasn't bothered by Fred's stylistic issues over fences. She encouraged Lisa to start showing him, even though his flat work was a work in progress.

After only a few weeks at Fairfield, they went to Florida and began showing Fred in the schooling jumpers. He was intensely allergic to wood, overjumping the 3'5" fences by two feet! It didn't take long to move him up to the high Preliminary classes. Fred usually jumped clean, but his poor turns cost him time in the jump-offs. Still, they placed regularly, picking up sevenths and eighths.

In Florida, Lisa had a chance to approach George Morris for advice about Fred. George determined that they needed yet more flatwork, something that appealed to neither Lisa nor Fred. It was like a required course in school that neither one wanted to enroll in. Both preferred jumping.

As Fred was very strung-out, George recommended a lot of counter-canter work to help balance his frame and shorten him.

Fred's wood allergy meant that he would stop rather than

jump out of an awkward distance that might cause him to hit a rail. Lisa didn't want stopping to become a habit, nor did she want to have a crash, particularly with a horse as sensitive as Fred. As the fences grew bigger and the courses harder, the chances of a crash increased.

Lisa needed to design a show schedule for Fred that was a training program as well in order not to discourage him, and to let him learn as his adjustability and turning improved.

She began the season in big fields with wide turns and long open lines, avoiding classes in small rings. Among Fred's extensive list of things that bothered him was bad footing, so Lisa only showed him when the footing was good. By never putting Fred in a situation that was wrong for him, he learned to trust her, and became very solid.

The following summer Leslie felt that Fred was ready to move up to the Intermediate Division, at Lake Placid. The footing was good, the wide grassy field was just what Fred liked. All the flat work had paid off. Fred was more adjustable and turned better. They won several classes.

Lisa had known her horse had potential. As he started to win more and more, she was encouraged by his success. But she didn't really know just how far he could go.

At the end of the year, Lisa needed corrective surgery on her knees. She'd wanted to slow things down for Fred a bit, so the timing worked out well. While she recuperated, Fred had six months off at a local farm in Arizona, just eating and enjoying his turn out.

The rest did him good. He returned to work more filled out and relaxed. When it was time to start showing again, however, Lisa realized that she had a problem. Fred had only competed at Intermediate for a short while, and she didn't think he could start up again at that level. Yet he had won his way out of the Preliminary division. She found a solution in a division held out west that was a transitional class between the Preliminary and Intermediate divisions, the Modifieds.

The conditions were just right for Fred. Classes were held

in large outdoor rings or big fields, with open, galloping courses. Fence heights were about 4'3". The modified division became Lisa's goal as she and Fred worked their way back to fitness.

Lisa continued with her canter and counter-canter work, and tried to get Fred to be more relaxed when jumping. Using low fences, or even poles on the ground, Lisa frequently stopped or backed up after the jump.

The Modifieds were an instant success, with Fred winning classes at every show. And Lisa learned just how Fred liked his warm-ups to go. Starting with a 3' vertical, she would work up to a 4'3" fence, with the ground lines rolled out properly.

Never fond of trotting jumps, Fred would just stop at even the lowest fence. Lisa simply learned to start the warm-up at a canter. Unlike other riders who might let a horse bump a warm-up fence in order to make the horse jump clean, Lisa would never consider that. Fred was so careful that if he hit a warm up fence, he'd be so upset he would stop at the first fence on course.

That September at Griffith Park in Los Angeles, Lisa decided Fred was going well enough to enter him in the Open division. He won. Encouraged by other riders and trainers, Lisa entered him in the Mercedes International Grand Prix. A World Cup qualifier with a daunting course, the move was not to be taken lightly. Still, Fred was confident after his recent wins. Lisa went for it. They won.

Always listening to her horse, Lisa decided that they'd done enough for the year.

Lisa planned for the next year to be Fred's first full year of competing in the Open Division. She got derailed by the news that he had qualified for the World Cup Finals in Gothenburg, Sweden. Still very inexperienced at this level, she didn't realize that she should have declined. Fred just wasn't ready. It turned out to be a disaster.

Home from Sweden, Lisa and Fred survived yet another disaster. In an Open class at Del Mar, California, Fred and Lisa competed at night under the lights. The light and shadows on the course confused him and he stopped several times.

At this point, Lisa realized she needed professional help, and arranged to work with Judy Martin, a trainer she had met at the shows. Lisa went home to Arizona for additional knee surgery, while Fred stayed with Judy.

Complications from the surgery prevented Lisa from riding Fred more than a week or two at a time, but it was enough to make it clear that Lisa needed to make some changes. Judy worked on Lisa's balance, making sure she did not get ahead of him. Lisa also needed to use more right leg. Unfortunately, it was her right leg that was recovering from surgery.

Judy wasn't quite so forgiving of Fred's quirks as Lisa had been. She considered him a spoiled brat whose owner had been letting him get away with way too much. They worked to get Fred to take more responsibility during the ride. Needing to compress his frame and shorten his stride to be competitive in the bigger classes, they worked on exercises to teach Fred how to do it. A pole on either side of a small vertical forced Fred to adjust his frame without Lisa having to use her hands.

Next up were tight lines with small jumps. These lines helped Fred learn to be comfortable with awkward distances. He soon learned that he was more comfortable when he shortened his frame.

When they began the new show season, Fred was feeling much more broken on the flat. His more adjustable stride gave Lisa options in a line instead of just going forward and leaving strides out. He also felt more comfortable about rocking back as he jumped verticals. Still, the turning problem persisted. Lisa knew they couldn't win in a small ring, or indoors.

Her new goal became to be able to turn Fred well enough to be competitive at any venue.

Qualifying again for the World Cup Finals, this time held in Berlin, Fred and Lisa headed to Europe once more. This time there were no stops, as there had been in Sweden, and Fred's more adjustable stride made the big, technical courses much more rideable.

At home, they were third at the Seattle Grand Prix. In the fall, she and Fred competed in the grand prix at Flintridge. The ring was much smaller than they were used to, and the Conrad Homfeld designed course was tough, with massive jumps and tricky distances. Two horses went clean in the first round: one was Fred. A careful, clear jump-off round produced a win!

The successes made them up their game plan for the following year. Lisa thought they might be able to qualify for Harrisburg, Washington, and New York. The indoor circuit took the Open jumpers who had earned the most money: Harrisburg the top 40, Washington the top 25, and New York the top 15. Earnings are counted from the previous September, and Lisa and Fred had had a good fall.

The first show of the year did not start well. Lisa withdrew from the first Grand Prix because of deep mud. In an Open class, Lisa had a bad fall at a skinny gate when Fred stopped for no apparent reason. He stopped again when the skinny gate made an appearance in a later class. Then, he reverted to his old habits: hollowing his back and running at the jumps. Lisa realized that he was panicked by his stops and her fall, but she couldn't figure out why he had stopped in the first place.

At the next couple of shows, Fred stopped several more times. Suspecting there was some other reason for the stops, Lisa had him reshod. The farrier found a badly bruised sole.

Although Lisa discovered that they had once again qualified for the World Cup, she passed, choosing instead to focus on qualifying for indoors.

They entered three grand prix at Griffith Park: they won two and were fourth in the World Cup qualifier. A few weeks later, a good placing at Flintridge meant the dream was falling into place. They were qualified for all three indoor shows!

The rings at the shows of the indoor circuit are tight: not the big, open fields that were Fred's preference. More leverage was needed to provide better turning in these rings. The D-ring snaffle was traded in for a gag bit that was wrapped in tape in order to feel more like the fat snaffle that Fred was used to.

Fred proved a star, placing third in the Harrisburg Grand Prix, and second in the President's Cup in Washington. An invitation to compete at the Royal Winter Fair in Toronto with the USET was extended.

Things had changed. Lisa knew now that she and Fred had a reasonable chance to win *every* time they entered the ring, not just when conditions were perfect for Fred.

Fred got some well-earned down time after Toronto. Lisa planned to show him in Arizona again, as it was the only time her family got to see them compete. After that they planned to continue to Tampa to compete at the Invitational, and try to qualify for the World Cup finals again. Lisa and Judy used information they had gleaned from riders who'd previously competed at Tampa, and tried to build similar situations in courses, so he and Lisa would be prepared.

Fred did his family proud, winning two grand prix in Arizona. Arriving in Tampa with weeks of showing under his belt, he was confident. The course for the Budweiser American Invitational, although not the biggest they'd faced, posed many questions involving lengthening and compressing of stride. Lisa didn't even have the opportunity to watch other riders go as she was third in the order of go.

All the flatwork and practice they'd done paid off. Lisa carefully followed her plan and they were clear, one of only 5 out of the 35 original competitors. It was outstanding competition: the other four clear were Rodney Jenkins, Joe Fargis, Greg Best and Jeffrey Welles!

The jump-off course again required adjustability and well-executed turns. Lisa, the second to go, knew that there was no playing it safe. She had to be fast with such a field of superstars following her.

As she started her round, she considered going for the easier option in the first turn. "No," she decided, "I came here to win!" Lisa left out a stride, took the faster routes, and galloped when she could. Fred was completely responsive, right on board with the tight turns and the need for speed. They went clean, and Lisa knew it was their best round so far in their time together.

Lisa couldn't bear to watch the others jump off. She and

Fred returned to the barn area. She heard all the others drop rails until there was only Rodney left. Then a groan from the crowd signaled she had won; Rodney's horse, too had taken down a rail.

Lisa and Fred were the only clear round. Fred was on a roll. And the second place horse, Olympic gold medalist Touch of Class, was *two full seconds* behind Fred's time!

Their win qualified Lisa and Fred for their trip to Paris for the 1987 World Cup Finals. Although Lisa set her goal there to finish in the top ten riders, Fred decided to up the ante. A clear first round saw them through to a hotly contested jump-off, which included Katharine Burdsall and The Natural (the eventual winners), and Paul Schockemohle on Deister. Lisa and Fred finished with four faults, in third place.

Lisa says, "He jumped *amazing* there. He had started to get very consistent in 1985 and 1986, and then when we won the Tampa Invitational, our first major event, that led to the World Cup."

The results in the World Cup led them to a spot on the Pan American Games team, held in Indianapolis, Indiana in 1987. When she and Fred helped the American team win a Silver Medal, Lisa says, "I started to realize that Fred *was* the horse that everyone said he was." That year Fred won six grand prix in a row, a record at that point.

After the successes of 1987, Lisa decided to go for the Olympics, to be held the following year in Seoul, South Korea. She was still in college in California, and it had never crossed her mind, or her family's, that the Olympics were a possibility.

She made the decision to keep Fred on the East Coast, with Michael Matz, while she flew back and forth from California. It was a difficult decision. She had always taken care of Fred; it would be hard to leave him. But all the big shows (Harrisburg, Washington, the Garden, and Toronto), were on the East Coast, along with the trials for the Games. There wasn't an option.

The process of qualifying in 1988 "was a nightmare. There were six trials, and you had to do all of them. We went to Old

Salem, Devon, Ox Ridge, Lake Placid...it was very stressful, and required a lot of jumping.

The whole process back then was that you were just observed by a panel, which put you in an order. I was the underdog, but I had a really good horse."

After all the trials, a short list was announced. The finalists went on to the Hampton Classic. "The finalists were all really good; we had a lot of depth...Rodney Jenkins, Michael Matz, Anne Kursinski, Joe Fargis....

When the selection process was all said and done, it was a relief. It was a long year."

But the Olympic Games were worth it. "They were fantastic! They were very well run and the facility was really nice. It was a great group of people, and the horses jumped really well. The jumps were beautiful, the weather was great. The courses were very hard. No matter how much you prepare yourself for it, it's just not the same.

For sure it was one of the highlights of my life, to be with all those people at that level of their athletic sport. I ran into Carl Lewis. You're in your own little world; you have to do a reality check."

Lisa and her teammates composed a real dream team. The other members were Greg Best and Gem Twist, Anne Kursinski and Starman, and Joe Fargis and Mill Pearl. The team took home a Silver Medal, with Greg and Gem Twist garnering the Individual Silver.

In 1991, Fred won the American Grand Prix Association Horse of the Year award, a feat he replicated in 1994. He and Lisa joined a second Olympic team, competing in Barcelona, Spain, in 1992. At 21, he won the Budweiser Show Jumping Championship in Wellington, Florida, the oldest horse to win a Grand Prix. In 2005, Fred was inducted into the Show Jumping Hall of Fame (along with Michael Matz).

Lisa says, "He was for sure my horse of a lifetime. He was a cool horse; he lasted until he was 24 or 25 when I retired him. We went to two Olympic Games, and he competed all those years without an injury. I spent my whole life with him. We went everywhere and did everything together.

He was a winner. It takes more than talent, it takes heart, it takes desire. Every time I went into the ring with him, I knew I had a chance to win. He was a show horse, and he was my best friend."

⟶ SWEET 'N LOW

It was 1983, and it was the record that almost didn't happen. Although Anthony D'Ambrosio prepared for it, and believed he and Sweet 'N Low could break the Puissance record, setting records is never an easy task.

Anthony knew he had a good horse, a horse possessed of tremendous scope. Sweet 'N Low had an almost freakish ability to jump high, and wide. But he would need every ounce of that ability in order to break the 7' 6 ¾" set by Glandor Akai and Barney Ward.

So they prepared. During the weeks prior to the Washington International Anthony and his wife Michael schooled Sweet 'N Low over six feet, and a little higher. Using the wall they had at their home farm, they practiced the massive heights in order to give the horse a reminder of the technique involved.

Sweet 'N Low, a 17.1 hand Thoroughbred who had run unsuccessfully at Waterford Park, among other tracks, was discovered by top horseman Vince Dugan. Jack Rockwell, a Connecticut professional, bought him from Vince for a client. The horse was always high strung and nervous, but Jack was very patient in bringing him along. Sweet 'N Low was sent to Terry Rudd for a period of time, and she did a great job of taking him to a higher level, what was then called the Intermediate jumpers. From Terry, Sweet 'N Low came to Anthony.

Anthony discovered that there were some issues that needed to be worked out, such as Sweet 'N Low's fear of water jumps. But it was always clear that he could jump like few horses in terms of sheet scope. He had placed in some of the biggest Grand Prix of that time, but never higher than third. He did score a big win, the Ben O'Meara, at the Washington International the previous year,

1982. It was at that show as well that Sweet 'N Low and Anthony had their first crack at the Puissance, where they tied for second with Danny Foster and Kahlua at 7' 1". Although Anthony knew that Sweet 'N Low could jump higher, he thought it unfair to ask him to try for the record in his first Puissance class.

But here they were in 1983, and this time back to win it and break the record. They were prepared; they had the ability. Anthony studied the Steve Stephens designed course for the first round. It was, as always, posted by the in-gate. Puissance courses are very simple, as the main objective is to clear the last fence: the big wall.

As they entered the ring, Sweet 'N Low could feel Anthony's excitement. The horse knew that this was an important round. They jumped clear.

Or so Anthony thought. Yet he had distinctly heard the bell in the middle of his round. Why would the judges be signaling him to stop? He wasn't off course; he knew that. There were only a few fences so it was close to impossible to go off course in a Puissance class, and Anthony had memorized the course perfectly. So he'd ignored the bell and finished his round.

As they left the ring, he heard the announcer explaining that Anthony had been eliminated for being off course. Jumping off Sweet 'N Low, he handed the horse to Michael. She was furious! How could Anthony be so stupid as to go off course in a Puissance? Anthony headed straight over to where the course was posted.

The course was different. There was an extra jump, one Steve had obviously penned in. The copy machine had cut off one of the jumps, and just prior to the class Steve had added in what he had intended. But no announcement had been made, and Anthony had felt no need to re-check the course when he knew perfectly well what it was.

Anthony asked to see a Steward, and explained his position. He had looked at the course when it was posted, and planned accordingly, and then went to help Michael tack Sweet 'N Low up and get ready for the class. If there was no announcement made, why would Anthony look at the course again? The Puissance class has the simplest course of all, or so one would think!

Could it be that after all this preparation, and with such a talented horse, that the battle they had to fight was not one of clearing tremendous physical hurdles, but instead the seemingly insignificant hurdle of an incompetent office worker?

After much consultation between the Stewards and the Judges, judge Frank Chapot came to give Anthony their decision. He said that at the end of the first jump- off, Anthony and Sweet 'N Low could come back and jump the entire course again.

"Why should I have to jump the entire course again?" Anthony asked. "I only missed one jump."

Frank patiently explained that he had gone to bat for Anthony with the foreign judge, so pressing his luck was not an option.

At this point, the first jump-off was almost over. Anthony ran up the ramp to tell Michael—who was still fuming because she couldn't believe he'd gone off course in the Puissance—that they were in fact still in the competition. As fast as they could, they threw the tack on, getting back to the arena with no time to spare, and he and Sweet 'N Low jumped the first jump-off again.

The announcer explained what had happened, and the audience got behind Sweet 'N Low and Anthony. Anthony will never forget the support, the cheers of the crowd, and the standing ovation as Sweet 'N Low again went clear.

In the next round, Sweet 'N Low was clear again. And on that October day in 1983 they set a new record of 7' 7 ½". The record has never been broken.

⌐ BORN TO RIDE

O ne of Tina Konyot's colleagues says "She rides beyond competition, with an excitement that emanates from her and broadcasts to those watching that something brilliant and extraordinary is taking place."

It's hardly a surprise. Tina Konyot has horses—and performing—in her bloodlines. Dating back five generations, her family has trained horses, danced in ballets and performed in circuses. Tina was born to ride.

Her grandfather, Arthur Konyot, performed for Ringling Brothers and Barnum and Bailey circuses, and trained horses for celebrities such as Arthur Godfrey. Her grandmother, Manya, was a Russian ballerina who practiced dressage as well. Father Alex was born in Budapest, Hungary, while her mother, high wire artist Josephine Berosini, came from Pilsen, Czechoslovakia. The two met in Liverpool, England when their entertainment worlds intersected.

Photos of Tina show her sitting as a baby in front of her father's saddle as they rode. Tina loved it from the start, heading for the stable the second she got home from school. Tina's riding took a "take no prisoners" approach. She rode with no hands, no saddles, and sometimes with an umbrella if it was raining. For Tina, "It was more comfortable for me to sit on a horse than to sit on the couch."

Growing up Tina rode with her dad, who ran a riding school in Fort Lauderdale, Florida. His reputation as a "genius with horses" attracted top-notch riders and horses to his school. He taught many greats in his 80-year career, including a very young Robert Dover. Robert says, "He was a genius who gave me key information at a very crucial time in my development as a rider."

Tina rode pony hunters, and pony jumpers, often practicing bareback with no hands. At 12, she was doing tempi changes and riding piaffes and passages on her father's horse. As Robert told her, "Nobody can get what you had in your life."

Later, Tina rode with Herbert Rehbein in Germany who she says was "her biggest influence in the competitive world of dressage." Other teachers included Rudolph Zeilinger and Klaus Balkenhol.

Even today she slides off the back of her Grand Prix horse, Calecto V, when she's done riding. Her horses are not competitive machines; they are her pets, her friends. It's not all about the sport to Tina; it's about the relationship. Her horses get to be horses: they roll around in the mud, take sun baths, go out on trails and get ridden bareback.

Tina still has her first dressage horse, now 28 years old, as well as another former competitive mount, 19. Along with a donkey, they wander around loose on Tina's property. Calecto can look forward to the same future. "I'll have him as long as he lives."

Tina first spotted Calecto (she calls him "Smoochy") at an auction in Denmark. He wasn't outrageously expensive, so he was affordable. But he wasn't ridden well and didn't sell. In fact, there wasn't one bid on him.

He did, thought Tina, have a beautiful canter and a nice walk. She rode him five times and ended up purchasing him a few months later. The man who bred Calecto felt that it was a great match, that Tina could make something special out of the horse.

It wasn't a decision most people agreed with. In fact, the consensus seemed to be that he would never go far. No one else had any confidence in the horse's ability. In fact, some other competitors were heard to say that he wasn't a horse that they would worry about competing against.

They were wrong. Tina says, "To buy an expensive Grand Prix horse and ride it well is great. But to bring them up on your own and do well, that's in a different league, a league all of its own. When you do that, you create such a bond between an animal and a person." She cites Ashley Holzer and Pop Art as an example.

Tina is incredibly proud of Calecto, and of how far he has come. When she got him, "He had no personality. He just stood in a corner with his head down. He had ulcers and was quite thin when I got him because he wouldn't eat." Calecto came from a huge breeding farm with over 600 horses. He was nothing but a number at the farm.

Now, says Tina, "Calecto is a changed horse." He comes out of his stall "very, very fresh. He's a totally different animal." With his weight gain and muscle, he's "twice the size of when I bought him, and he has so much personality. No one can believe the change in him!"

In fact, he became so much horse that at one point Tina thought to herself, "What am I doing?"

Tina's philosophy is evident in her teaching as well as her riding and performing. "It's all about being fair to the horse. Sometimes miscommunication can occur. It's not fair to the horse. You have to be clear and people should be as quick to reward when the horse earns it, as to punish."

When working with her horses, Tina says, "Every horse is an individual. What their issues are every day is different." Some days she'll take it easy and just go on a trail ride. Other days, she asks more of her horses.

Tina's overall goal is to "stay happy and healthy on a daily basis, to keep my horse happy and healthy, and to enjoy my life."

Tina is proud of Calecto at every show. Riders who thought they had nothing to fear from Calecto have been forced to sit up and take notice. Among Tina's proudest moments have been winning the Grand Prix Freestyle at Dressage at Devon and taking a second in the Grand Prix there, breaking the 70 % barrier in the Wellington Classic Spring Challenge CDI, and qualifying to ride for the United States in the World Equestrian Games.

Qualifying, says Tina, "felt fantastic, it's what you work for." It was the first time she rode for her country. "I felt honored; it's a very special achievement."

Riding on a team is, naturally, different than riding for

yourself. "You want to do well for your team." Tina was lucky in the fact that teammates Todd Flettrich and Katherine Bateson-Chandler are friends, so there was a comfort zone for all of them. And she enjoys the atmosphere of competing with all the other disciplines on the same grounds. In that way, "It's similar to Europe."

She was disappointed in her own rides. "I knew I could have done better. We did so well at Aachen; it was very, very special to be in the top ten in that company. But at WEG I rode my horse off his feet in the Grand Prix special. You live with it, you don't dwell on it. You have one extra cocktail that day and then you learn from it and go on."

Tina has definitely not been dwelling. Recently, at the World Dressage Masters in Palm Beach, she and Calecto finished with a second in the Grand Prix and a third in the Grand Prix Freestyle.

It's not solely Tina's, and Calecto's, talent that makes them stand out from the pack. FEI Olympic judge Axel Steiner says, "There are many riders, but there are only a very few who are true partners with their horse. Tina is one of them."

Rocky sticking his head into the front seat while riding in the truck

Lisa picking up baby Rocky at the airport

Rocky riding in the truck

Lisa Kelly's Rocky

Rocky and Travis watching TV together

Rocky dressed in costume

new born Skye and her mom Sara

4 months old

Lisa Kelly's Skye growing up

Lisa Kelly and her beloved Skye reunited

Padré
Photos: Chuck Swan / Swan Studios LLC

Gunners Special Nite (Bailey)
photo: Diana De Rosa

For the Moment
at Barcelona and Seoul Olympics
Photo: Tish Quirk

Sweet 'N Low and Anthony D'Ambrosio
setting the indoor record of 7' 7½" at the
Washington International Horse Show
Photo: Pennington

Calecto V and Tina Konyot
Photo: Diana De Rosa

FAMILY

⟶ CHARMANDER

They don't come any cuter. With his tiny ears, thick forelock, and delicate Welsh pony face, Charlie is irresistible. He struts when he walks, proud of his job of carrying small riders, and well aware of how well he does it.

Charlie (Charmander) was bred and born to be a champion hunter pony. That was the idea. His dam, Three's A Charm (registered name Fine Design), was a top contender in the hunter world, trained at one time by pony legend Emerson Burr.

When Three's A Charm retired, she was bred to a top pony sire, Pendrocks Sir Percy, by her trainer, Kathleen Byers.

Three's A Charm died shortly after giving birth to her son. The orphan foal was carefully fed milk replacement to insure that he got the necessary colostrum (the first milk mammals produce, which contains antibodies to protect newborns against disease). Charlie was bottle fed, and grew up thinking the humans feeding him were his parents. He has since always maintained that he is human.

Like his mom, Charlie moved beautifully and jumped like a star. Although he was meant by Kathleen as a show mount for her daughter, things didn't work out as planned. Charlie was carefully brought along and took to training eagerly, but Alura had only begun showing Charlie when she sprouted upward so fast that she quickly outgrew his small frame.

Charlie, meanwhile, impressed everyone in the barn. His sweet nature endeared him to all who crossed his path. He knew he was meant to be a star, and there are a lot of ways to shine.

Kathleen, who had been working out of Millbrook Equestrian Center, moved to Oblong Valley Stables, to work for Michael

Chamberlin and Margie O'Brien. When she began teaching their daughter Elizabeth on Charlie, it was a natural fit. Lizzie loved Charlie and Charlie loved Lizzie.

The Chamberlins, smitten by the pony as well, purchased him for Lizzie. Charlie became the foundation for their farm, the whole reason the entire family has since become obsessed with horses. Anyone new coming into the barn is introduced to Charlie. "It's his barn," Michael explains to visitors.

The Chamberlins now own a barn full of eventing horses, show horses, and a young horse, Dilly, who Lizzie is proudly starting herself.

Charlie's show career started well, carrying young Lizzie to many co-championships, or reserve championships, in the walk-trot and then short stirrup divisions. Tragically, plans for pony hunter classes were cut short by a lack of Vitamin E, causing Charlie to have muscle weakness which prevented him from showing and jumping.

As the saying goes, when one door closes another one opens. Charlie's show career was over. But Charlie's happy and outgoing personality, his need for interacting with people, his patience and understanding of small beings were all still there.

Just because he couldn't show didn't prevent him from changing lives.

Gianna Cice was born with a love for horses. Her parents, Chris and Roseanne, have no idea where it came from, but Gianna is very clear on the matter. Nothing is as important to her as horses. Before she'd even celebrated her second birthday, her bedroom was littered with stuffed horses that she could sit on and ride, books about horses, and model horses.

All that was good up to a point, and it was even better when Gianna's parents took her for rides on the merry-go-round at the Danbury Fair Mall. But Gianna knew that that was just a temporary fix. Only the real thing would do. Her parents, along with her grandparents, Evelyn and Joe Cice, got it. They arranged for her to go a nearby barn, the Chamberlin's Oblong Valley Stables.

There she would meet Charlie and Tucker.

Gianna is by nature a very happy and loving child. But meeting a horse and a pony in one day? She was overcome with delight. First she met Tucker, one of the stunning Thoroughbred residents of the farm. Although a little taken aback by his size, she was thrilled to be so close to a real live horse!

Next, Charlie was led in. Gianna's eyes lit up, but she still wasn't quite sure she should get close to him. She hid behind her father, peeking out from behind his legs at the adorable pony. But actually touching him? Now Gianna wasn't sure. The pony was far bigger in person than all her stuffed animals.

Charlie looked at Gianna patiently. Feeling her hesitation, he didn't want to scare her.

Gianna inched close to Charlie, but not close enough to touch him.

Slowly Charlie stretched his head and neck nearer to the tiny human. Gianna didn't move. In slow increments, Charlie grew closer as he lengthened his neck. Soon, gently, he touched Gianna with his soft pony nose. Gianna's whole face lit up with pure joy. Soon she felt secure enough to pet him, and softly brush him. Then her father lifted her on to Charlie's back.

Gianna's parents had never seen anything like it. Their daughter couldn't stop smiling and laughing. She was living a dream come true.

But wait, something was missing! She was sitting on Charlie bareback. Where was the saddle? Only three years old, and she'd never met a horse before, but Gianna knew. There was supposed to be a saddle!

Charlie was returned to his paddock, and Gianna and her family went out for lunch. Giddy with excitement, Gianna couldn't sit still. She circled the table, played on the floor, and ran around the restaurant.

She couldn't stop talking about Charlie.

She talked about Charlie, and about Tucker. Every night she asked her parents to tell her bedtime stories about Charlie, and about Tucker, the beautiful horse.

Gianna had had the chance to sit on Charlie. Merry-go-rounds no longer stood a chance. Yet she and Charlie hadn't gone anywhere. She knew she had to go back; this time she would *ride* Charlie.

Her family returned to the barn, and this time, there was Charlie...with a saddle on him!

On this visit, Gianna fed Charlie treats. Putting her fingers right into Charlie's mouth, she slipped the treats to him. Charlie gently extricated the cookies from her hand, careful to separate food from fingers.

Chris placed his daughter on Charlie's back (on the *saddle*) and Gianna was led on Charlie around the property. There was no fear this time. She sat proudly and confidently, amazing her father with her confidence about the whole situation.

"She's a natural!" he exclaimed in wonder.

Charlie marched up and down the driveway, thrilled to be introducing another little girl to the joy of horses, and proud to be doing what he had been born to do.

⟶ BETELGEUSE

Joanne Bundy had dreamed for years of a chestnut Quarter Horse. Gelding, of course. Joanne loves geldings and already had two mares.

Now she was in search of a horse "for her old age." The time had come to make her dream come true.

Joanne had been a fan of the stunning stallion Obvious Cash for years. His get were consistently lovely horses, easy to work with. So Joanne's search began, and ended, with a trip to see some of his youngsters. She spotted a handsome chestnut colt and a striking filly. In fact, the filly "was to die for." But it was a gelding Joanne wanted. Snapping a photo, she returned home to her husband.

Joanne's husband Al lay on the couch when Joanne walked in the door. Showing him the photo, she told him, "That's your new son."

"I don't want to hear about another horse," he responded.

The task of picking up the dream horse fell to Joanne's daughter Laurel, along with her friend Marie. Marie had just purchased the chestnut colt's half-brother. It sounded like a simple assignment, but it came with major complications.

The babies had just been weaned. In fact, they had just been weaned on the day that Laurel and Marie arrived. And the seven-month-old colt had been introduced to halters a mere hour before they showed up to take him to his new home.

That was just the beginning of their troubles.

Loading two babies who have never been on a trailer before proved, as may be expected, frustrating and time consuming. It took much longer than they'd thought it would, but finally they got under way.

Marie had worked for a time shipping horses for a commercial hauler, so she was naturally at the wheel. It didn't take long for things to go from bad to worse.

As the trailer started to make its way down a hill, Marie inquired if Laurel had her seat belt on.

"Of course I do; I always wear my seat belt," Laurel replied.

"Good," said Marie, "because we have no brakes."

Laurel thought instantly of the babies in the back. Her mother's dream horse! How was she going to tell her mother that she'd killed her dream horse! That was, if she survived to tell her.

Besides, Marie had just put new brakes in the truck. How could they not have brakes? "But I thought you'd just put in new brakes!"

"I did."

New brakes or not, they weren't working.

Marie's years of experience professionally driving horse vans allowed her to remain calm. Cell phones were not yet in every pocket, so Marie drove the brakeless rig while using her CB to notify the fire department in nearby Walton, New York, that a runaway horse trailer would soon fly into (and through) town. The department turned out to be a godsend, quickly blocking roads and clearing any impediments to a safe landing for the trailer.

Marie may have remained calm, but Laurel clung to her seat frozen in fear. An impromptu roller coaster ride (with horses along, no less) was not her idea of what the day's activities would bring.

Marie brought the truck and trailer safely down the hill and to a stop in town. Not only did she stop it safely, but she placed it impeccably: right next to a gas station, where the truck could be repaired!

Fire department officials and townspeople immediately appeared to make sure everyone was safe.

The first thing they wanted to do was unload the horses.

"No way!" Laurel told them. "They're babies; we'll never get them back on!"

So the truck was unhooked from the trailer and went to the

gas station for repairs, leaving the babies still in the unattached trailer.

Word spread fast and soon people started showing up left and right with hay and water for the horses. Soon so much had arrived that the two babies could have been fed for a year!

Meanwhile Joanne and Al were waiting for the horses to arrive. Laurel called her father from the gas station to let him know what had happened, and he agreed to let Joanne and Al know that Joanne's dream horse wouldn't be home any time soon.

It took eight hours before the truck was ready for its trip home. The exciting adventure of going to pick up two new horses had turned into a long, terrifying, and arduous assignment.

When the new horse finally made it home, he was as yet unnamed. Naming a new horse can be challenging, which explains the number of defaults one encounters to such old standbys as Star, Red, and Socks.

The task fell to Laurel's father Bruce, and no run of the mill name would be applied to *this* horse! When Bruce and Joanne were married, Bruce spent weekends at Hayden Planetarium teaching astronomy to youngsters. Laurel and her brother spent a lot of time playing at the Planetarium when it was closed. Her brother loved to scare her, playing such pranks as turning on the Mammoth exhibit when Laurel wasn't looking.

Bruce loved astronomy, and Joanne's new horse with his bright chestnut coat and regal bearing looked like a star. He named the gelding Betelgeuse, after the brightest star in the Orion constellation.

"Juice" might have looked like a star, but he didn't begin his career acting like one. His lunging lessons were disastrous. Juice broke three of Laurel's fingers in the process of learning to lunge.

After that, Juice began to act more like his illustrious sire. Juice was a joy to break, and a joy to ride. He was "so easy," says Laurel, "the easiest horse I ever broke. The only challenge was the way he kept growing, he'd be uphill, then he'd be downhill, then he'd be uphill again." With all the constant height shifts, it took

Juice nearly six years before he evened out.

Laurel had a tiny young girl, Pam McCarthy, help her start Juice. Pam's mother and grandmother both told Pam, "*No*," she wasn't to ride and help start a young horse.

Pam apparently didn't hear, for she says, "My most favorite childhood memory was starting Juice."

Juice picked up the correct leads from the beginning, and his lead changes were automatic. Anyone could ride him. And everyone wanted to. In addition to his great mind and the good education he received, his gaits were heavenly.

Juice fulfilled his promise and is now a wonderful old age horse for Joanne. He'll do just about anything he's asked. Pleasure classes? He's never been less than reserve. Hunter paces are a favorite for him; dressage is fine too. Swimming? Sure! Just point him at a lake. Juice just aims to please so whatever Joanne or Laurel want is fine with him. Going down hills is one exception. Juice hates to go down a hill and will buck to make sure you get the point.

Joanne and Laurel are quick to credit Juice's disposition to Obvious Cash. All of the stallion's babies are "just plain easy." And Joanne is quick to credit her horse for all the successes they've shared. "It's just Juice. He's so easy. He always knows just what you want. He's always been such a sensible horse, so dependable."

Trainer/judge Ken Fairfax broke Obvious Cash…when the stallion was 20. Asked what he did, and how did it go, Ken said blithely, "I just got on."

In addition to the pleasure classes, Juice has placed in many paces, and was third in his first dressage show. Juice has been so successful, so calm and willing, that people constantly come up at shows and hunter paces to see if he might be for sale. "No," answers Joanne, "he's for my old age."

Once, Joanne took Jane, a very timid rider, on a trail ride at Wethersfield in Millbrook, New York. All Jane wanted to do was walk, and that proved a tad boring to Juice. Still, he didn't argue. Most horses would have gotten frantic at the others galloping ahead, or trotting by. Not Juice.

The confidence Jane gained through Juice has changed her life. No longer timid, she now canters and jumps small fences, and has gone to, and placed in, several shows and paces.

Juice's enthusiasm for life is boundless, and sometimes he pushes those boundaries. Playing in the snow one day, he injured himself badly, tearing a tendon in his right ankle. Joanne and Laurel were devastated.

They were willing to try anything to help Juice get better. They tried shock wave, but three shock wave treatments later Juice was still in pain and barely able to walk out of his stall.

They consulted an equine massage therapist recommended by Laurel's friend and student Jennifer Grant. The results, says Joanne, "were nothing short of a miracle."

After that Juice was so improved that he and Joanne went for a ride at "the track" in North Salem and then on the beach in Fairfield, Connecticut.

Marie and Joanne both say, "When you sit on one of these horses, you're so happy you can ride forever." That's a great thing to say about your "old age horse." Or any horse.

At one point Joanne discovered that, although she was all right getting on a horse, getting off was almost impossible. Her hip wouldn't let her. The time for a hip replacement had come. After the surgery, Joanne could not ride for six months. Laurel kept Juice worked for her.

When she could finally get on again, Juice, thrilled that his mom could ride once more, started bucking. Luckily, Joanne wasn't quite on yet. "He's not as quiet as I was hoping for, for a 75 year-old lady."

But she's not complaining. "I can't ask anything more of him. He's taken me so many places, and done so much for me."

Charlie as a foal

Charmander

Charlie and Alura

Gianna feeding Charlie a carrot

Charlie and Lizzie

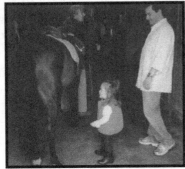

Gianna Cice and her dad Chris Cice
at Oblong Valley Stables, Gianna is all
ready to go for a ride on Charlie.

Betelgeuse

Rescues

⟶ CASH STARS AND BARS
"VINNIE"

Born to be a pole bender in Rockford, Illinois, the little Paint apparently didn't look like a leading contender. As a yearling he was placed on an auction truck, and the outlook was not promising.

Sande Shamsh purchased "Cash Stars and Bars" and another yearling from a friend who had rescued them off the truck, fearful of their final destination. He took the two young horses to a farm in Antioch, Illinois.

Later, Sande left the farm and moved to North Hill Farm in Spring Grove, Illinois. Unable to afford board on more than one horse, he was forced to leave Cash behind, taking only his own horse CK.

A year later, when he discovered that North Hill's manager, Polly Hall, was looking for horses, he was able to return for Cash. He found the young Paint in decent shape, but basically unhandled.

Cash moved into North Hill in May, 2006, and Mairi Thennes remembered her first impressions of him. Standing alone in the small paddock next to the barn, the Paint was quiet and reserved. He came to Mairi at the fence, and together they stood for a long time, at least half an hour. To Mairi, he felt like an old soul, which was something people always said about her son Alex. Ever since Alex was a baby, he had been quiet and calm, exhibiting a Zen like quality.

After being given a chance to acclimate to his new life, Cash (now named Vinnie) was started under saddle. Eleven-year-old son Alex had begun to forge a friendship with Vinnie, so he was elected to put the saddle on the young horse for the first time. Polly instructed Alex to let go of Vinnie if he started to panic. She wanted to be sure Alex didn't get hurt.

Alex began walking the young horse around the farm to get him used to the new gear. At first, Vinnie didn't seem to mind. But when the young Paint stopped to investigate a wheelbarrow of dirt, he snorted at the contents, kicking up dust. Startled, Vinnie took a sharp breath and felt the girth tighten around him. Panic at this strange thing cinching his mid-section sent him running and bucking.

As a matter of pride, Alex tried to hold on as Vinnie bucked around the farm. With everyone else shouting at him to let go, he eventually conceded and released the Paint. Vinnie quickly calmed down, finding the grass more interesting than his freedom. Little did Alex know that this was just the start of adventures with Vinnie.

The rest of Vinnie's "breaking" proved uneventful. A working student at the barn, Jenna, found him very easy to train to ride.

By September, Alex had begun to ride Vinnie. Although cooperative for the most part, during a fun show at the barn in October Vinnie's pole bending breeding took over during the running of the bareback obstacle course. Alex leapt on to his back from the mounting block, and Vinnie took off running and bucking down the long side of the arena. This time Alex didn't manage to hold on.

But all ended well.

Alex had been riding an off-the-track Thoroughbred named Clarence, and Mairi and her husband Allen hoped to buy the horse for their son. Clarence had some eventing experience, so Alex would be mounted on a horse with mileage. Things didn't work out the way they had planned, but they did work out the way they were supposed to.

The family that was interested in three-year-old Vinnie experienced a change of heart. Vinnie had contracted rain rot, and the mother began riding Clarence. Falling in love with him, she purchased him instead. Since the Thennes had not yet mentioned their desire to buy Clarence, they lost out. Instead of the more experienced horse they wound up with three-year-old Vinnie.

It wasn't just his age that made him seem an unlikely choice. As Mairi says, "Vinnie was the last horse I would ever have purchased based on his appearance. An almost entirely white, butt higher than his withers, three year old. But this quote always comes to mind, 'A good horse is never a bad color.' I believe the quote is from Monty Roberts." When people comment to Mairi about how white Vinnie is, and what a pain it must be, she tends to recite that quote.

Mairi was right to be concerned over Vinnie's unbalanced conformation. It would prove to be the source of many difficulties. But although she felt a little guilty because they hadn't planned to buy Alex such a green horse, Alex eased her concern about Vinnie. A bit of a computer geek, Alex explained that Vinnie was "like an unformatted computer; he can be anything I want him to be."

Alex seemed to instinctively understand that this was the right way to go, so the whole family embraced the new direction of "green project horse." And the "project" would include building a better boy: Alex. Alex would do the work, and train Vinnie from the ground up. He would have weekly lessons and Polly would be there to guide him, but she would not do the work for him. It was a lot to ask of an 11-year-old boy, but the Thennes feel that "success is much sweeter when you have done it yourself."

Rather small at 15.1 in the front, and a little taller in the back, Vinnie is almost entirely white with a few small patches of sorrel. His size, however, is no reflection of his attitude.

One eye is partially blue. His large nose has a black dot on one end. Most people would not consider him a pretty horse, but as they come to know him, Mairi says, "his physical attributes fall away and you see him with your heart. We of course think he is the most beautiful creature on the planet."

Very quiet and well-behaved under saddle, Vinnie is terribly naughty on cross ties, lead lines, and lunge lines. Breaking cross ties is a much-practiced sport, lunging is an opportunity to show off his pole bending speed, and hand walking is nothing more than permission granted for a bucking spree.

The Thennes fondly refer to Vinnie as a "freak" because he is so conflicted within himself. Vinnie will chase a coyote out of the field, yet cower at a saddle pad; joyfully run in the rain, but bolt at the sight of the wash rack. "Perhaps," says Mairi, "it is all the same, maybe he is just extreme. His love is big, his loyalty is big, his joy is big, and he has a very strong flight instinct."

Alex has learned not to question it anymore, choosing simply to embrace Vinnie's quirkiness and channel it in a good direction.

In the spring of 2007, Vinnie's downhill conformation began to take its toll. Vinnie became lame. Although the lameness subsided, he still was "not quite right." He was short behind, and felt like a sewing machine when Alex rode him. It took the Thennes, Vinnie, and several vets over a year and a half to work through the issue.

Vinnie constantly tested everyone. Between that, and his physical issues, Mairi's and Allen's hearts broke for Alex. Would their son ever realize his dream of eventing with Vinnie? Yet Alex's fortitude astounded them. He kept trudging forward, wearing a smile on the outside and believing in his horse. It made it easier for the Thennes to believe, as well.

Vinnie was crooked in his hips, with the left hip protruding higher than the right. Blocking, and then injecting, his hocks helped somewhat. More significant improvement resulted from chiropractic treatment with Dr. Mike Buskohl.

Over time, Vinnie's front end began to catch up to the back half, which eased the crookedness issues.

As Vinnie turned four, and Alex reached 12, the team began showing in some dressage schooling shows. Although not the most successful endeavor, it provided some good learning experiences. Numerous challenges greeted Alex, including foals that so fascinated Vinnie that he could not focus on the test, and terrifying bridles that caused rearing episodes. Alex continued to be patient, focusing on the journey.

One summer morning Vinnie came in from turn-out with what appeared to be tree sap all over his nose. Unwittingly the Thennes tried to wipe it off. What they were trying to wipe off, it turned out, was ooze from a severe sunburn! Everyone felt terribly guilty that their attempts to "clean" his nose only intensified his suffering.

When the vet arrived, Vinnie was cowering in the corner of his stall and wouldn't let him anywhere near. Alex soothed him, allowing the vet to treat him.

Haltering and bridling, difficult before, now became a constant battle. Alex quietly worked through this obstacle the same way he had dealt with previous ones.

Although her son's slow progress with Vinnie frustrated Mairi, she came to see that it was no accident that Vinnie came to be theirs. Vinnie and Alex were meant to be together. Alex seems an "old soul" with his calm demeanor and belief that everything will work out all right, a "yang" to Vinnie's "yin." Their relationship is explained well by this Taoist creed which maintains that these complementary opposites interact within a greater whole as part of a dynamic system. Vinnie needs Alex and responds to Alex's reassuring manner. Although he can always be counted on to register his opinion on things, in return Vinnie generously displays athletic ability for Alex that seem far beyond the possibility of his small, limited body.

His constant testing of Alex, pushing his buttons and waiting for a reaction, has proven beneficial for Alex. All the challenges Vinnie has presented Alex with have created a better horseman, a better person. The journey of "building a better boy," has, in Vinnie's head, been about building a boy of steel!

Still working with the short stride issue, Alex and Vinnie began showing in combined training in the spring of 2008. But Vinnie cast his vote on dressage arenas in no uncertain terms, leaping from the ring sideways when circling at "A."

Although several methods were employed to try to change

Vinnie's vote, nothing succeeded. At event after event, Vinnie and Alex were eliminated for ducking out of the dressage ring.

Fortunately, they were only competing in a schooling show series and most judges were kind enough to let them compete in the jumping phase even though they'd been technically eliminated.

In the fall, they entered their first Mini Event (an unrecognized event which follows all the same rules as one which is recognized, but in a more relaxed environment). Alas, the dressage ring struck again!

This time, however, the outcome was different. The judge, Adrienne Pot, invited Alex and Vinnie to come back and complete their test even though they'd been eliminated. Scoring the entire test, she let Alex compete in the other phases.

Vinnie has never left the ring since. Mairi says she owes Adrienne Pott "a debt of gratitude."

Although the duo finished 2008 without much show ring success, things were coming together. Vinnie was moving well again thanks to the injections, the chiropractic treatments, and the fact that his small body had grown more balanced.

As spring of 2009 approached, the Thennes family wondered, "Will this be the year? Dare we dream?"

All winter Alex and Vinnie had worked hard, practicing their dressage. It was starting to look like something, and the judges took note. At the first mini event of the year, they ended up tied for first. The tie, broken off of the dressage free walk, placed them second overall in the pre-novice division.

At the next event, the success continued. They won!

They won the next event, as well. Moving up to beginner novice mini events, the success continued.

In fact, they were so successful that they qualified for the 2009 Illinois Dressage and Combined Training Mini Event Championships in both Pre-Novice and Beginner Novice divisions. Competing in the Pre-novice division, they won the championship!

The ugly duckling had blossomed into a champion.

The 2010 competitive season was late in starting for Vinnie, as he sustained a suspensory injury in January. For three months, Vinnie remained on stall rest. Cooping him up turned Vinnie into a tantrum throwing terror. Hand walking him proved to be an exercise in self-preservation for the humans at the end of the lead shank.

Finally, in mid-May Vinnie was back in work and competed in a small hunter show. He jumped right back onto the fast track to success, as though the whole lay-up had never happened.

After all the success of the previous season, it was time for Vinnie and Alex to move up to Novice Level Mini Events. Not only did they qualify for the IDCTA Mini Event Championships at that level, they won: at a level two divisions higher than the division they had competed in and won the previous year.

Alex was excited about moving up to recognized events the following season. He and Vinnie had paid their dues and had come a long way on their journey together. His belief in Vinnie had been well founded. The horse could be anything Alex wanted him to be, and now he truly was an *eventer*.

Then came the phone call that every horse owner fears: an early morning call from the barn. Just four days after Vinnie and Alex won the Novice Mini Event Championships, Mairi was jolted by Polly's message on the answering machine. Although her voice was calm, Mairi read the underlying tone. Something terrible had happened to Vinnie.

Unable to reach Polly, Mairi bolted out the door in hysterics. Racing the 20 minutes to the barn felt like an eternity. Phoning Allen to pick up Alex from school, Mairi told him she didn't know what was wrong, but Vinnie was either dead or dying. Since Vinnie trusted Alex more than anyone, it was crucial that he come. And if there were decisions to be made about Vinnie's treatment, Alex needed to be involved. Should Vinnie have to be euthanized, Alex needed to be there for Vinnie, and for himself.

At the barn, Mairi found Polly walking Vinnie in from the field. The injury, thank God, wasn't as serious as she'd originally thought. She'd been sure that Vinnie had cut the suspensory ligament of his back leg, and would have to be destroyed. Still, Vinnie was limping significantly, and had a horrifying gash on his left rear leg.

"How can he even be walking with that?" Mairi wondered.

The gash was so deep that the cannon bone was exposed, and it was over a foot long.

Vinnie had been found trapped in wire when Gerardo, one of the barn workers, went to bring another horse in from the pasture. He had managed to wrap a braided tension wire around his leg. Gerardo found him on an incline, wedged against a fence, lying on his back with his head pointed down.

Polly was forced to use bolt cutters to cut the thick wire from Vinnie's leg to free him. She was amazed when Vinnie, freed from the wire, promptly got up, and wandered off, rear leg dragging, for a drink and to pee.

Dr. Tully from Elkhorn Vet Clinic arrived, followed shortly afterwards by Alex.

A quick examination revealed that all the tendons and ligaments were intact, although the sheath to the extensor tendon might be nicked. The cannon bone literally had saw-like markings from the braided cable. The vet felt that Vinnie must have lain there for six hours. He was amazed that Vinnie was patient enough to lie still, and amazed as well that he somehow managed to miss all the critical structures.

Alex, as always, astonished his mom. While she had reacted by panicking, he remained calm and collected throughout the ordeal. This helped keep Vinnie quiet as he was cleaned and bandaged.

Although no one is sure how Vinnie managed to wrap a tension wire of that gauge around his leg, they do know that he was spared for a reason. He was not finished with Alex yet.

Vinnie was stabilized, and taken to Elkhorn Veterinary for further treatment. For four days he received intravenous antibiotics and was watched carefully for complications from his ordeal.

When he returned from the clinic, constant bandaging and

antibiotics became part of the family routine. Initially it took the three of them 45 minutes to bandage Vinnie. By a few weeks down the line (and a switch from wet to dry bandaging) Alex could do it himself in five minutes.

Finally after two months, the cannon bone was completely covered by tissue and the bandaging nightmare was over. The nasty scar that remains is a reminder of how lucky he is to still be here, and how resilient he and Alex both are.

In 2011, Alex and Vinnie returned to competing, doing a recognized Beginner Novice event at Fox River Valley Pony Club in June. They went right back to the head of the class, winning their division over a large field, and qualifying them to compete at the American Eventing Championships. Moving up to Novice Level at a recognized event, they placed third.

Now, Alex was forced to make a decision. He'd hoped to compete with Vinnie at Richland Park Horse Trials in Michigan, a CIC*** event that is not limited to the upper levels. Instead the event includes Novice through CIC***, giving the lower level riders a chance to ride with the "big guns," an opportunity Alex very much wanted to take advantage of. But now they were qualified for the championships! They couldn't do both, as the events were spaced only two weeks apart, and it would have been too much for Vinnie.

The championships took place in Georgia, 800 miles away. Vinnie had never been on a trailer for more than 40 miles. Richland was four hours away. Although the length of the trip concerned them all, Alex decided to go for it and compete at the AECs. The little rescued Paint had qualified for the national championships, and he deserved a chance to show what he could do!

Just for fun, "Team Vinnie" brought along "Fat Stanley," a stuffed toy horse, to be their mascot. Taking photos of Fat Stanley as they passed through different parts of the country, they shared them with everyone who was cheering Vinnie on back home. Even their vet was on their email list of people to update.

It lifted Alex and Vinnie up to know that so many people

were sending them good thoughts, and it was thrilling to share this very special part of their journey together.

Arriving in Georgia, Alex and Vinnie were scheduled for dressage the following day.

Unfortunately, considering his predominantly white coloring, Vinnie hates the wash rack with a passion. He refuses to go in, and if he does manage to get dragged in, immediately drags his torturer out again. Even after five years of working with Vinnie with a wash rack (using an inordinate amount of bribery), Vinnie remains no fan of the device. In preparation for Georgia, where there would be an outside rack, the Thennes spent a month acclimating Vinnie to being washed outside. Week one was torturous for all concerned, but by the end of the month Vinnie was handling it well.

So, they thought they were prepared. *Wrong.*

Vinnie became so unglued at the wash racks that the Thennes were forced to wait until the racks were clear of other horses before daring to risk a confrontation and embarrassment. Then they had to wrestle with Vinnie for an hour trying to get him washed.

Considering his coloring, a successful bath is critical. The Thennes are forever grateful to their dear friend Judy, always a big fan and supporter of Alex and Vinnie, who presented them with a bottle of "Wow"™ prior to their trip to Georgia. That bottle of Wow™ was a godsend, preventing future wash rack battles at the AECs. After the bath on Thursday, they just used Wow™ spray to touch up his dirty spots for the other competition days. No one believes they could have survived another bath!

Dressage day arrived, and it was evident from the start that good things were going to happen. Alex and Vinnie's ride time was 9:11 a.m. on 9/9/11 as the world approached the 10th anniversary of 9/11. Alex is the son of a veteran firefighter, riding a rescued American Paint Horse named Cash Stars and Bars. The coincidence of it all was overwhelming.

Mairi's eyes filled with happy tears when she saw the times. It meant good karma, and it felt very significant although also surreal. Alex, of course, thought it all quite silly. He didn't need good karma. That's what he had Vinnie for.

Always it is the dressage test that makes Alex the most nervous at events, and often the resulting nerves create problems. Alex is aware that Vinnie's pole bending genetics do not serve him well in the dressage arena, but he wants desperately for the world to see what he sees when he looks at Vinnie: a lovely, quiet, obedient horse with a huge and generous heart. He therefore puts a great deal of pressure on himself to try to make that happen

Despite those nerves and couple of resultant bobbles, Vinnie took care of things. The test was respectable, placing them sixth out of 67.

Team Vinnie was thrilled! Their first goal had just been to get Vinnie to Georgia without a major incident or meltdown. Then they had set their sights on finishing in the top 50%. For the duo to have made it to the top 10 blew their minds! They hadn't dared dream of such a result.

Throughout the day, numerous texts and calls came in from everyone back home who was following the live scoring online. Everyone's best wishes were aimed at the little underdog of a horse.

Vinnie's ground manners have always been a bit suspect, and on Saturday he decided to start the day by goofing off. Polly had the early morning shift for Vinnie's care, and after feeding and watering him, she'd decided to take him for a walk around the grounds. The walk turned into a Wild West rodeo display at the end of a lead rope. Although Mairi concedes that the theatrics come under the heading of naughty behavior, she would never take that spark away from Vinnie. "I think it is that little bit of fire in his personality," she says, "that gets him around the cross-country."

A beautiful, rolling, cross-country course awaited Alex and Vinnie. One of the questions on this course was a drop off of a bank, on the side of a hill. Drops are the elements which concern Alex the most. Vinnie doesn't "drop" off of anything, instead preferring the crouching tiger leap into water.

There was a water element to ride through as well. Although Alex and Vinnie have worked on water for years, it remains a challenge for them. Vinnie pitches a fit to avoid going into water, yet, once in, he loves to play and doesn't want to leave. So Alex is faced with a double-edged sword: he has to not only get Vinnie *in* the water, he has to get him *out* as well!

On course, the duo headed for the water and although Vinnie ducked and dived a bit, he went in, and trotted through it. A few more easy obstacles under their belt and the dreaded bank loomed ahead. Although Vinnie didn't drop nicely off the bank as hoped, he didn't play crouching tiger either. Always prepared, Alex stayed in the "backseat" just in case.

The rest of the course remained uneventful and they finished on time with no jumping faults. The clean round moved them up a spot into fifth place and on to the stadium phase.

A fairly straightforward stadium course included bending lines and a roll-back at the end. Vinnie bumped one rail, but it stayed in the cups and the round was clear.

Four horses remained to jump the stadium course. The horse in second place dropped a rail: Vinnie and Alex had moved to fourth.

This proved especially lucky, as it meant a white ribbon instead of a pink. It is difficult enough to be one of the few male riders at the lower levels of eventing, without the added insult of a pink ribbon. Still, the team would have been thrilled at any ribbon!

A lovely awards ceremony followed the show jumping, with ribbons presented by Mr. Bouckaert, the owner of the Chatt Hills facility. While all the other horses stood quietly when their ribbons were pinned to their bridles, true to character Vinnie objected, backing and ducking out of reach.

Alex finally had to ask Mr. Bouckaert to hand him the ribbon, which he hung from his boot. As they took their well-earned victory lap, Alex couldn't just relax and savor the sweetness of success; he had to fight to hang on to the ribbon hanging from his boot!

But it was all worth it and nothing short of a miracle. Their rescued bred for pole pending American Paint Horse, with all his physical and mental challenges, had overcome everything to place fourth at the American Eventing Championships.

.

⟶ SAMPSON

Sampson started out life unwanted, as nothing more than a by-product in the production of Premarin. Luckily for Sampson, there are caring individuals and organizations out there that exist to save the lives of horses like him.

In 2005, United Pegasus, a rescue organization out of Tehachapi, California, shipped three tractor trailer loads of these "by-products" from the PMU ranch in Alberta, Canada, to safety. PMU stands for "pregnant mare's urine," from which Premarin is derived. Many PMU babies end up on European dinner tables.

Initially named Freckles, the sorrel colt was one of 25 weanlings who came through United Pegasus across the country to Equine Angels in New Milford, Connecticut. By a Percheron stallion named Corbin, Freckles is out of a half Belgian, half Quarter Horse mare named Raspberry. The four-month-old colt was neither halter broken, nor handled. Mia Genovesi took Freckles home, along with three other weanlings, to begin the long process of acclimating him to humans, halters, stalls, and other life lessons.

Mia runs Godspeed Horse Hostel, Inc., a horse rescue in Amenia, New York, and has a lot of experience with PMUs. Most people would not be able to adopt an unhandled part-Draft horse directly, as they would not have the experience to bring one along. Mia has a system she has honed over the years that works very well, and Freckles fit perfectly into that system. He turned out to be one of the easiest babies she had ever worked with.

Mia refers to her program as "The Art of Not Training." She spends a great deal of time just "being" with the babies. Initially the babies live out, with a run-in shed. They are fed three times a day, and Mia interacts with them twice a day in addition, grooming and petting them and just sitting with them. When they are older they come in to be fed, in order to become accustomed to a stall.

Mia's program, like so many horse rescues, benefits people as well as horses. Mia started a horse treat business in order to raise funds for the rescue. The treats are manufactured by kids from Maplebrook School in Amenia, a school for kids with learning disorders. Some are autistic kids, who become far more social after being exposed to horses. Other kids come from the school as part of a work-study program, to help on the farm. Skill levels for all school subjects increase in those participating in the program, for the kids learn that doing a good job is crucial to the horses' survival, and the importance of doing a good job carries over to their schoolwork and life skills.

Although the horses in Mia's program are initially shy, eventually their curiosity gets the best of them and they begin to approach her. In time they learn to love being groomed. The progress continues to leading, clipping, blankets, trailering, and beginning lunging. Usually Mia keeps them until they are about two years old, and then sends them off for saddle training with natural horseman Bob DeLorenzo in Middle Grove, New York.

Mia says her program is "like boot camp, it's very consistent."

Freckles traveled with Mia to Tennessee, where she moved after the expected sale of her New York farm. When the farm didn't sell, Mia had to move back to New York. She didn't relish the idea of taking the six rescues she currently had with her back to New York so she looked to find homes for them. At the time, Freckles was four years old and a star graduate of her program.

Since Mia feels that rescue horses are the public's horses (some of the funding for the horses comes from the public), she has made it her goal that they should serve the public. As a result, she has teamed up with therapeutic riding programs, and Intercollegiate Horse Shows Associations programs, to donate the rescued horses to them. Two of her other horses, Lana and Girlfriend, went to the Sacred Heart Therapeutic program in Sparta, Tennessee.

She contacted nearby Sewanee College, but at the time, they had no room for another horse. So she gave Lynn Petr of Shangri-La Therapeutic Academy of Riding (STAR) in Lenoir City a call. STAR is one of only a handful of five-star rated facilities in the country and has several programs including Heroes and Horses (a therapeutic riding program for veterans), Changing Strides (for at-risk youth aged 13-21 to better manage their lives and foster positive relationships through partnership with a horse) and Minis in Motion (to expose more people to STAR and Equine Assisted Activities by traveling with the miniature horses to schools, rehabilitation centers, nursing homes or camps).

Lynn was hesitant. "We don't usually take horses that young," she told Mia.

Mia insisted that Freckles was special. "He's different; he's one of a kind."

Lynn agreed to come and take a look at him. Freckles passed their initial evaluation, and went back to STAR for a three-month trial. The trial only lasted two months. "We definitely want him," Lynn told Mia.

Although Freckles (whose name was changed to Sampson as there was already a Freckles in the program) was much younger than a horse they would normally take on, Lynn says he was "a laid back guy, and always in your pocket. Mia had put professional training into him, and because of his upbringing, size and training, he was worth the time it would take for us to ease him into our world." It was also quickly determined that Sampson would be a perfect fit for the "Heroes and Horses" program.

"He makes a connection quickly with people," says Lynn, "and he's a good solid size for the men he needed to carry."

Sampson has been an amazing success. In no time he became one of the most requested horses in the program. He tolerates the overhead lift required to put people on him from their wheelchairs. He puts up with blowing bubbles, noisy or wiggly riders, and rings on his ears, tolerating many things that other horses find intolerable. His attitude is not "*Oh my God what's that?*" but rather a curious, "Whatcha got?"

Lynn says, "It takes a while for 'stop' to go through from his brain to those huge feet. He's slow and methodical, which we need. We need a horse that stops and looks rather than one that is very reactive."

Sampson can be used on-lead and off-lead, which many of the other horses can't do. He is an easy keeper requiring little food, and goes barefoot without a problem. He is an amazing asset, with the ability to take care of the lowest functioning, to the most capable riders. He is "a soul who is so easy to be with for everyone: riders, instructors, and volunteers."

Sampson is also a "spokesman" for PMUs, educating people about the torturous conditions that the mares live under, and the slaughter that awaits so many of the babies. Although there are now far fewer ranches due to the exposure of the health risks that women taking Premarin are subject to, and the barbaric treatment of the horses, it is still an issue that needs to be resolved.

A custom western saddle was created for Sampson, something that certainly isn't done for every horse. But Sampson was so valuable that he earned it. He is also so tolerant that he can be used with just a pad and a surcingle.

For the Heroes and Horses program, it is important that the veterans become engaged. Part of Post Traumatic Stress Syndrome is the desire to get away from everyone. Many of the veterans lock themselves away in their homes. Sampson draws them out. One program participant came every week to work with Sampson. When he was with the horse, he developed a calm countenance. Lynn would often see the two of them with their foreheads pressed together. "He can calm that battlefield; calm that mind," she says.

There are breaks when the Heroes and Horses program is not in session. It didn't matter to this man. Even when it wasn't in session, he came just to see Sampson.

Marilyn, one of the instructors at the program says, "I love having Sampson in my classes, whether on or off-lead. He is such a gentle giant, and mature for his age. When 'A.B.' rode him off-lead, they made quite a pair: he made her work to apply aids correctly, and *always* responded quietly. He has great endurance, which is a wonderful aspect of having a young, strong, and fit equine companion."

Marilyn also reports, "Sampson is unflappable, too. 'M.M.' can get very excited. Last session we did lots of games like 'Float the Duck,' where she trotted with a cup of water and giggled loudly the whole time. He gamely absorbed all the activity, and seemed to enjoy the huge hug she gave him afterward. To be honest, I am disappointed when Sampson is not in one of my classes; I love him!"

Another rave review came from instructor Catherine. "My favorite Sampson story is from last winter when 'W.C.' had a seizure while riding Sampson. Although Sampson is sometimes wiggly and curious, he seemed to understand that he needed to be totally still. Sampson squared up, and although wide-eyed, stood like a statue during and after the seizure when we needed to dismount his rider. I was very grateful for Sampson's understanding that night...Sweet Sampson!"

A few months later a student was walking while waiting for his turn to dismount. Suddenly the horse leader called out to the instructor that Sampson wouldn't move. She tried and tried, but he stood stock still. The side walker then noticed that the rider was having a mild seizure. When the seizure subsided and the rider was asked what his horse's name was, he said loudly, 'Sampson' and at that Sampson moved off at a slow, steady walk.

"That," said the instructor, "is the definition of a special animal."

It may have taken Mia a little while to convince Lynn that Sampson belonged in her program. But now all Lynn wants to know is, "Do you have another one like Sampson?"

To volunteer for, or donate to, Mia's rescue, go to
www.godspeedhorse.org. Mia can always use donations
of wormers, horse supplies, etc.

⁓ THE NATURAL

Some of us spend our entire lifetimes trying to determine what we want to be when we grow up. Others figure it out before they grow up.

As a very young child, Caroline Heitmann of Clinton, New York, used to watch her brothers ride their horses. In time, she decided that this was something she wanted to do as well. Her brothers soon lost interest, but Caroline was hooked.

Caroline learned to ride on Taco, her trainer Meghan O'Brien's horse, but it didn't take her long to want a horse of her own. Make that *horses* of her own. She soon had three of them: Heavenly Hudson, a Haflinger, and two miniatures, Ever So Clever Eddie, and Small Sacrifices Scotty.

Hudson came from the New Holland auction, notoriously known for selling horses for slaughter. Starved and ill with strangles, Hudson was presented as a two-year-old gelding. It turned out he was only a weanling (and a colt at that), but Caroline's mother Joanne calls him "the best mistake I ever made."

Scotty came from upstate New York, in the Troy area. Unhandled and left out to pasture until the age of three, he was then adopted and gelded by a local woman. Unfortunately the woman's pony did not get along with Scotty, and Caroline was chosen to be Scotty's new owner.

Eddie was found through a free horse advertisement that Caroline and her mom saw on craigslist. They were uninterested in the mares posted on the list, but went to meet with the owner to educate her about giving away horses, and what would most likely happen to them. Just before they left little Eddie popped out from behind the run-in shed, and there was just no way to leave him behind!

Hudson from the start proved to be a sweet and curious guy who would follow Caroline and Meghan everywhere. His kind personality made him very easy to work with and teach. Although he was young and unhandled when Caroline got him, with Meghan's help he has come a long way. Last year Caroline showed him (as a yearling) at the Dutchess County Fair in Rhinebeck, New York in Showmanship in the Draft Horse division. This year, competing in their first performance division, Caroline and Hudson ribboned in their very first class. Despite being at the Dutchess County Fair, with all of its distractions (carnival rides, concerts, crowds), Hudson focused on his job, performed beautifully and didn't spook at anything. Caroline was so proud; she says "He was just awesome!"

Caroline plans to break Hudson to ride in the spring.

Eddie, although a stallion, is quite mellow. Before the Heitmanns purchased a trailer, they would just stick Eddie in the back of the car to take him somewhere. Eddie would look out the window as they drove. He now has learned to drive, pull a cart, and to jump as well.

Scotty proved to be the tough one. Caroline wanted to teach him to drive but he would often try to bite, or kick her when she tried to put on the tail piece of the harness. At first Scotty was so frightened he wouldn't work with anyone but Caroline. When Caroline's father tried to help her give him a bath, Scotty attempted to run away. Another time when her father was home alone Scotty escaped, and he ended up chasing the pony all around the yard to catch him. It wasn't quite what he'd planned to do with his day.

That's all changed now. With the help of Caroline's 4-H leaders, Lenny Miller and Stephanie Weber Fitzpatrick, Scotty has come a long way. Caroline took Scotty to 4-H horse camp, at the Dutchess County Fairgrounds. Scotty got his first driving lessons here, and then went on to compete at the Dutchess County Fair. Caroline just wanted to try it "because it would be a good experience for both of us."

She had little idea how it would turn out.

Competing in the Draft Horse events, Caroline and Scotty

won first place in Ground Driving and first place in Showmanship. In the Ground Driving Obstacle Course (where participants must weave their horses through such obstacles as cones and barrels, cross over a wooden bridge, and go around an umbrella), they placed second. She and Scotty were competing against teams with vastly more experience together than they had.

Initially, Caroline was given the Reserve Grand Champion placing, but it was discovered that the score had been incorrectly tallied. They were actually Grand Champions!

Caroline's goal with her minis is to do weddings with a little cart that she has (Eddie is already happy to pull it) bringing flower girls and ring bearers into the ceremony. That's just the beginning. With all this success so early (Caroline is only 11), she has no doubt that she wants to become a professional horse trainer.

And her parents? They love the idea. "We think she'd be really good at it!"

⟶ SPARKLE

BonnieJeanne Gordon first noticed "Sparkle" when she and her husband were walking through the auction building before the sale began. Spotting the small white mule, she saw a "devil's glint" in his eye.

"You should be named Sparkle," she told him.

BonnieJeanne hadn't planned on bidding at the auction. As her husband had never been to an auction before, he had asked if he could go to one to see what it was like. But as he and BonnieJeanne sat in the audience, the little mule came up for sale. BonnieJeanne realized that the man bidding on the mule was a buyer for a slaughterhouse. Unwilling to let that happen, she ripped a number out of a nearby person's hand and stuck it in the air.

BonnieJeanne went home with the mule for $125. He was promptly named "Sparkle." The 14.1 hand mule was three years old, and basically unhandled. Used to living in survival mode, he proved a major challenge to everyone at BonnieJeanne's Tara Farm. Sparkle didn't understand that Tara Farm was a sanctuary, a safe place, and so he remained on high alert.

His primary means of maneuvering was on his hind legs. Sparkle would drag anyone who tried to lead him, letting them know who was in charge. He broke things on the trailer. He was impossible for the farrier (BonnieJeanne gives farrier Matt Lewis a great deal of credit for sticking with Sparkle), impossible for the vet. The shell he had built around him was about three feet thick and he had no intention of letting anyone get close to him.

Luckily for all his theatrics, mules are tough and don't get hurt as easily as a horse. They are extremely good at self-preservation.

BonnieJeanne attended an Equine Affaire clinic given by a

natural horseman from Arizona, Steve Edwards, in which he taught attendees how to work with mules and donkeys. Mules are psychologically and emotionally very different from horses. They don't take kindly to discipline. Pressure points on these equids are not the same as on horses, so saddles fit differently, halters fit differently. A misbehaving mule or donkey may just be objecting to a poorly fitting halter. People working with mules and donkeys also have to learn to keep the animals' heads down, which helps keep them calm.

BonnieJeanne purchased a book about mules and donkeys, so that she could learn more and have a reference to deal with when she ran into challenges.

Given his sometimes violent misbehavior, BonnieJeanne decided that another horse might prove a good teacher for Sparkle. She put him in a pen with a horse that was half Belgian, half Haflinger. As BonnieJeanne says, "That horse just put him in his place."

Tara Farm doesn't only rescue animals. BonnieJeanne finds that it works both ways. Although all the animals are rescues, they seem to be pretty good at rescuing people. "Animals," she says, "are amazing for healing the soul and the spirit."

BonnieJeanne pairs animals with kids in combinations that she feels will be most effective. Sparkle became Heather Jordan's project. As an unpredictable animal, not just anyone could be paired with him. Heather, a local 4-H kid, can be contradictory and stubborn, but she excels at working with animals.

Heather has always had an affinity for the more challenging cases. She doesn't give up easily, sticking it out when others might have quit. One pony that Tara Farm had rescued reared all the time when it came in. Thanks to Heather's work, that pony is now used on pony rides.

Heather spent hours doing groundwork with Sparkle. She experimented with a lot of different bits, and got run away with many times when she first started riding the mule. Sparkle is smart, which was sometimes helpful and sometimes detrimental. Discovering the difference between working with horses and mules proved to be a great learning experience for both Heather and BonnieJeanne. Both needed to learn patience: it was going to take time with Sparkle.

They had known from the start, given the glint in Sparkle's eye, that he was a little wise guy and things would never be predictable or easy.

Over the years, things improved. There are fewer bumps on the path. Sparkle has given Heather a tough time, but he's given her rewards as well. Initially, when people made fun of her for showing up with a mule at a horse show, she would get upset. Now she holds her head up high, proud of what she has accomplished.

Sparkle has gone on to learn dressage and jumping. At their first show together, competing in a Pleasure class with 22 other horses, Sparkle and Heather wound up first. Those who laughed at the little white mule couldn't help but notice. Judges always notice Sparkle (how could they not?) and are happy to share a word of encouragement with Heather. At one show a judge told her that she should be very proud of herself, as he could tell that Sparkle "has a mind of his own."

At donkey and mule shows, where the animals are shown in hand or in harness, Sparkle has won every time out. He also excels at "coon jumping."

In the past (and perhaps now as well), people would pack out on mules when they went coon hunting. The places they went were interlaced with stone walls and barbed wire. Going around the obstacle would take too much time. So the farmers would take off their coats, place them over the wall or over the wire, and the mule (or donkey) would jump the fence. The sport that arose was thus called "coon jumping."

Heather's work with Sparkle and the other rescues has helped mold her as a person. Heather is a redhead with a true redhead personality, but Sparkle has humbled her, teaching her patience and respect. In turn, she has done wonders with him, bringing out the talent in a wild and unpredictable animal. They have helped each other be the best that they can be.

Tara Farm rescues all kinds of animals. They are a sanctuary for FIV and Leukemia positive cats, and currently house potbellied pigs, llamas, chickens, rabbits, Chow dogs, goats, and of course various equines. Currently they care for *141* animals!

Many of their rescues can never leave because of medical issues. Other rescues have been adopted but continue to board there.

To raise funds, Tara does petting zoos, pony rides, and hunter paces in the fall. BonnieJeanne spends a good amount of time applying for grants. The facility needs updating, so there is always a lot of fund raising that needs to be done.

Many kids from single parent families come to Tara. Schools bring special education classes. Community service kids or adults help out. Tara Farm is not just rescuing animals but also educating the public, giving them a chance to be exposed to animals and to enjoy their company.

BonnieJeanne is very grateful for all the help they receive. Farriers and vets give breaks on their services; both Girl and Boy Scouts volunteer their time. Massage therapists have given the rescues free massages.

BonnieJeanne says "It is amazing to me what animals do for the kids. You see this energy level between them and a special needs kid, you see that the animals sense the need to be different."

BonnieJeanne's house is large, with many extra bedrooms. The rooms house residents, who, like the horses, have found themselves in need of a helping hand.

The combination of animals, and humans, needing help, never fails. Just like Sparkle's and Heather's lives were transformed, the four-legged and the two-legged help transport one another from fear and confusion to safety and confidence.

Tara Farm is located up on a hill, and BonnieJeanne calls the hill "Magic Mountain," because miracles happen here.

If you are looking to adopt a rescue, or want to know what you can do to help, contact www.tarafarmrescue.org.

Cash Stars and Bars (Vinnie)

Sampson

With adult rider and side walkers

*With independant walker and
Marilyn C., Instructor*

With Veteran

Heavenly Hudson

Sparkle

PERSISTENCE

NEVER UNDERESTIMATE A HORSE LOVER

Claire Fraise has always had an affinity for animals. As a baby growing up in New York City, Claire much preferred the company of dogs in Central Park to the endless humans surrounding her.

When George and Cath Fraise moved their family to Connecticut, they noticed an amazing change in their daughter. Now out in the country, surrounded by grass and trees and living things instead of concrete and asphalt, Claire blossomed.

The new lifestyle suited the whole family. George, who had done some competitive swimming in his youth, had a pool put in at their house on Tyler Lake so that the kids could learn to swim and become comfortable with being in the water. Little did he know where it would lead.

He taught Claire and her brother Tristan how to swim and how to tread water. Although George emphasized that treading water builds endurance, Claire found it boring. In order to make it a little more appealing, he enticed her with contests. If she would tread water for five minutes (with no use of her arms allowed) she would win a stuffed animal.

This made it a bit more interesting. Claire loves stuffed animals so she won it easily.

Besides swimming that summer, Claire was also taking riding lessons and going on trail rides at Lee's Riding Stable in Litchfield, Connecticut. Although initially Claire's pursuit of the sport was a casual one, in time she began riding the school pony Cinnamon. Riding Cinnamon proved a lot of fun and Claire's commitment increased.

As the treading water contests continued, George let Claire know that the longer she treaded water, the bigger the reward would be. Claire allowed herself to dream. If you're going to dream, why not dream big? "If I tread water for an hour, could I get a horse?"

George, positive that there was no way that would happen, agreed. "Yes, you could get a horse."

But treading water was so boring. "Can't I just swim for an hour? How about if I swim the lake?"

Claire was only eight years old and Tyler Lake was a good sized body of water. George envisioned years of training. Maybe in two, three years, Claire could swim that lake. That would mean a horse was years down the road.

So they started training, combining laps with treading water. That lasted a week, maybe two. Bored again, Claire asked, "Can't I just swim across the lake now?"

George knew she wasn't ready. She couldn't be fit enough. She would find out. So he agreed. He would canoe across so that when she tired she could grab hold of the canoe, and then climb in. Claire would not be allowed any flotation devices, and as soon as she touched the canoe the contest was over.

George and Claire had entirely different visions of the outcome. George was sure his daughter would be exhausted, climb aboard the canoe, and the quest for a horse would be put off for a few more years. In Claire's mind, there was absolutely no question. The horse was already hers.

The day of the contest arrived. George took off from one end of the lake in his canoe with Claire swimming alongside him. After no more than 50 yards, Claire admitted she was tired. It was just what George expected. "I figured you would be. Get in the canoe. We need to do more training."

He didn't realize that Claire had a secret weapon. Although no external flotation devices were allowed, Claire knew that her own body was a flotation device. She could conserve her energy by taking breaks, letting the water hold her body while she floated.

So she continued on. As they neared the middle of the lake,

Claire was visibly tiring. George thought it was over. He brought the canoe nearer to his daughter. "You look tired. Don't you think you should get in the boat?"

"I am NOT getting on the canoe!" Claire responded.

Now George found himself getting very concerned. They were into the second half of the lake! Could she really do it? And it wasn't just a matter of swimming across the lake. It was rough, with waves and wake from boats washing over Claire's head. She would emerge coughing and gasping for air.

She kept swimming. The other shore loomed closer. The next time George asked his daughter if she wanted to climb in, she noted the desperate tone to his voice. He kept nudging the canoe closer. "I think you should get in the boat now."

Claire was tired. But she was never tempted to get in the canoe. "I had it in my head that I was going to get across, and when you commit to something, you'll do it."

Claire didn't think about how tired her body felt. Instead she pictured the horse that was hers when she reached the other side.

Exhausted by the time she touched the far shore, she couldn't even walk. For an hour and twenty minutes Claire had been swimming. But it didn't matter now. The first thing she said to her father was, "My legs feel like rubber." The second thing was "So when do I get my horse?"

When she got home she went on Lee's Riding Stable's website and started looking at potential horses. Making her choices according to her favorite color (buckskin), Claire picked out a few possibilities. One of them was the beautiful young Morgan mare, Windfield Contessa. That weekend the family went to Lee's and spoke to Claire's trainer, Heather Johnson, about what horse would be good for her. Heather agreed that Contessa might be a good match, but she also chose another option, Oakley.

Oakley was cute, but he kept trying to pull his head down, and Claire, a petite rider, was not strong enough to control him. Contessa proved a much more agreeable ride. So, despite her father's teasing her about choosing a horse by its color, Contessa it was, and she indeed proved a great match.

Claire says "I love riding, riding for pleasure. I just want to have fun with her. I love hanging out with her." Although Contessa is only five and a bit spooky, Claire is learning to deal with it. "It makes you become a better rider. I help her improve and she helps me improve. I feel like it's a team effort whatever we do."

Claire loves it when she walks in the barn, calls Tessa's name and her horse picks up her head and looks for her, and nudges her pockets looking for carrots. Although she "loves any horse she sees," Claire's voice when she speaks of Tessa is radiant.

And George? Well, George will *never* make another bet with his daughter.

⟶ Ride of a Lifetime
The Tevis Cup

Ask any endurance rider what his or her ultimate goal is and the answer is always the same: to complete the Tevis Cup (officially known as The Western States Trail Ride). This grueling ride consists of one hundred miles in one day over the most challenging terrain any rider will ever face. Horse and rider teams that finish the course from the Robie Equestrian Park near Truckee, California, to Auburn, California, and are judged "fit to continue" are awarded the coveted Silver Completion Award buckle.

Ann Cofield had wanted to complete this legendary ride since she took up endurance riding in 1978. From 1978 to 1981 she competed in as many endurance rides as possible in the Southeast Region, read every book and article available about the Tevis, and concentrated on improving her riding. In 1981 Ann leased a horse and pre-rode sections of the trail with a local endurance rider in preparation for finally attempting the ride. Her dream ended for that year when the mare she leased caught her foot between some rocks, pulling the ligaments severely.

The experience made her more than ever aware of the tremendous effort involved in the endeavor, and how vital it is to have dedicated and knowledgeable help.

Returning to her home in Georgia, Ann "tried to put this conquest out of my mind." It didn't work. "The charisma of the trail became a siren call. I knew I would return!"

In the fall of 1985 Ann saw an advertisement for a four-day seminar on the Tevis trail to be held in July 1986, presented by Lari Shea. Knowing the Tevis crossed far more rugged terrain than most of the trails in her own Southeast Region, she decided to lease a horse for the seminar. Although Ann had never done a 100-mile ride before, she decided to make the Tevis Cup her first because, if "I did a 100 mile ride and found out I didn't like it, then I would never do the Tevis Cup."

The Tevis Cup's historic trail goes through Squaw Valley (the site of the 1960 Winter Olympics) up through Emigrant Pass, following a route used by Wells Fargo Express riders when they carried the mail and treasure for mining camps along the Gold Rush section of the trail. The nickname "Tevis Cup" traces back to Lloyd Tevis, who had served as director of Wells Fargo from 1872-1892. A description of the trail from the Tevis Cup website warns: "Adequate physical training and preparation for both horse and rider are of the utmost importance." Courage is also a highly recommended ingredient.

Inspired by the Pony Express (which despite its prominence in western lore, only lasted 18 months), the ride tests horses and riders to the limits of their endurance. Pony Express riders rode 100 miles (or more), however they changed horses every 10 to 15 miles. The route was so dangerous due to terrain, weather, and the threat of being attacked by Indians or robbers, that a help wanted poster for the Pony Express stated "Orphans Preferred."

Although today's riders can feel pretty sure they won't be facing bullets or arrows, they do face temperatures from 40-120 degrees Fahrenheit, dust so thick that the trail disappears, narrow paths along deep canyons, rocky terrain, and debilitating exhaustion. Some of the specific challenges of the trail include "No Hands Bridge" (a former railroad bridge, the narrow crossing has no side rails and a 150 foot drop on either side to the American River below) and iconic "Cougar Rock" (a large volcanic cone outcropping with a steep, narrow and treacherous passage over slippery rock—and deep canyons on either side).

To compete in the Tevis Cup, horses must be at least five years old; riders need to be 12 (children must be accompanied by an adult). Horses carry a minimum of 165 pounds. Most contestants ride Arabs or Arab-crosses. Arabs have been bred for stamina and speed for centuries by the Bedouins and continue to excel in this discipline. They also seem to have a natural sense for pacing themselves.

The Tevis Cup begins at 5 a.m. on a Saturday in July, and is timed to coincide with a full moon for riding at night. Riders are divided into groups of 10, and a group leaves every two minutes. There is a vet check on the Friday preceding the race to check pulse, respiration, and soundness. Riders are allowed to use any kind of tack and they do! There are several vet checks along the way, and it is always heartbreaking for competitors to get that far and then have their horse pulled. The vet checks also provide a chance for the horses to be sponged down by crews that meet the riders at the checks, rest, and eat some hay. The horse's pulse must drop to 68 pulses per minute and the horse must jog sound before being allowed to continue.

Here is Ann's story of her Tevis Cup adventure.

As we began our journey on the seminar that summer day, I was truly joyous to be on my way at last! We clambered over millions of rocks and traveled narrow dusty ledges. Redwood forests surrounded us as we made our way into deep canyons and over the American River. Around each bend in the trail vistas of the Great American West spread out before us. It was easy to imagine immigrants, gold seekers and pioneers seeing this very view and wondering what lay beyond.

At the seminar I learned more about horse care on the trail and pacing through the ride. Pacing was a major concern since this was to be my first hundred-miler. I made plans to return the following summer. I would lease a horse for the seminar and do the Tevis a few weeks later on that horse. I went back to Georgia light-hearted, on the edge of my dream.

During the following year I rode the trail many times in my mind. I felt a mental power building, stronger than I had ever experienced, and envisioned only success.

The horse I leased for my second seminar and the ride was Napoleon Redbird, a seven-year-old chestnut Arabian gelding. Redbird is a sound horse with a good disposition, and a lot of heart. The respect I have for this horse's endurance and intelligence is beyond words. *He* should be wearing the Tevis buckle!

As I sat on him waiting for the ride to begin, I felt an intense concentration. I reviewed in my mind only what I needed to remember from the start to Emigrant Gap. I knew I could lose it all in the first few miles if I couldn't control the horse's pace. Beginning an endurance ride with a horse in a snaffle bit always lends an element of adventure! My mind flashed back to one of my first endurance rides where we led the pace for a mile or so: out of control with a snaffle bit. Not a fond memory. But I felt I should trust Lari's decision about the horse's headgear and I would adjust.

The early morning darkness became electrified with sparks from the horses' hooves prancing on the pavement. The start made me nervous—so many excited horses in such close quarters. I worried that we might get kicked. I inched my way up to the gate and with great relief gave the timer my number. We were on our way!

Redbird trotted out briskly, but in control. I searched for a group pacing the way I had planned. The riders were spread out and I felt safe. We trotted on up to Emigrant Pass, walking intermittently to let the horses catch their breaths. I remember the advice given to me so many times: "Ride your own ride." The words echoed in my mind as these riders and I passed each other on the trial numerous times on our journey. After we had climbed for a while, I had a moment to take one last look back at the lights of Squaw Valley and to the sunrise over Lake Tahoe. The line of riders ahead, silhouetted against the early morning sky, and those below on their tiny horses with puffs of breath punctuating the air, gave me courage to ride through a day and a night, hoping my dream would not be crushed among the rocks again.

I felt a special bond with these people, the place in time, and our common desire to finish safely with a sound horse.

I wanted to reach Robinson Flat, the first vet stop, by 10:30 a.m. Aware that this would be a long, hard, rocky stretch, I rode cautiously. Redbird wore splint boots, but no pads. I knew he had good feet and prayed no rock had his name on it that day.

The horses traveled head-to-tail for what seemed like an eternity. Dust smothered the slow-moving line, snaking its way on the narrow trails toward Cougar Rock. I tried to be patient, knowing that later there would be time to move on.

As we neared Cougar Rock butterflies in my stomach reminded me of one of the horses I had ridden in the seminar. He turned around almost at the top and wanted to go back down! A real heart-stopper! But Redbird, with his expertise, climbed straight to the top without a misstep. I loved him more than ever. As we traveled across Red Star Ridge on the treacherous footing, I did have a few moments to enjoy the wilderness beauty. Then high above I saw a tiny silver plane, the only sign of civilization.

Before long, we reached the first manned water stop. I had the luxury of a pit stop for myself and felt better as I remounted. Redbird drank well and was alert but relaxed. The riders were spread out now and most of us were trotting along whenever possible. I enjoyed the people I met on the trail and everyone seemed in an "up" mood. "This isn't so bad," I thought to myself. As I remember, this was the last time I had that particular thought!

As we neared Robinson Flat, Redbird quickened his pace, remembering that this was one of our camping places on the seminar. What a welcome sight to see the vet stop and one of my crew smiling, and taking pictures of my dust-blackened face. At the two previous seminars I had met the Mundy family from Redlands, California. This summer they graciously volunteered to come and crew for me. What a joy to know I had my own special crew. They did a really professional job for a most appreciative horse and rider.

By now, we were thirty-five miles into the ride. I had arrived at the vet check at 10:45, only fifteen minutes off my estimated time. I felt comfortable with this, but realized I would have to keep moving at a steady pace whenever possible in case something unexpected happened. Redbird passed the exam with only a word from the vet. "Wash his nose out."

As we left Robinson Flat, Redbird looked longingly back at the vet stop, but soon was distracted by the other horses ahead of him. By the time we reached the long down hill road, I was anxious to trot again to gain a little time. My knees were in major pain, the non-stop kind. My concern was whether the pain would increase with the looming miles or level out to a dull ache. Fortunately it became bearable.

Redbird wanted to go faster and faster. Thinking of his legs, too, I tried to keep him at a moderate pace as I alternated posting and standing in my stirrups. At last we reached the bottom of the descent and stopped for water. Redbird was still drinking well and seemed stronger than ever. We continued trotting.

At the turn-off to Last Chance, we walked quite a distance and arrived there in good condition. Luckily, we got checked right away and were able to move on.

The next stretch to Devil's Thumb and the check at Deadwood would be one of the most taxing portions of the ride. As with many other riders, I would not see my crew again until Michigan Bluff. We trotted most of the canyon down to the river. Again, my knees complained, and now my burning feet as well. I reminded myself that aches and pains come with the territory of endurance riding and we trotted on. At the river we watered, crossed the bridge and began the long climb to Devil's Thumb. Some people "tailed" on their horses, but I did not, having no experience with this skill. There was only one other person and myself climbing together for a long stretch with no one close. We were able to rest the horses along the way. Even resting, plus pouring all the water I had left on Redbird's neck, he was sweating heavily. I could feel his sides heaving and felt he might be getting into oxygen debt. Not knowing what help I might find at the top, my plan was to rest there until he recovered and continue on to the Deadwood vet check.

What an unexpected and happy surprise when I came to Devil's Thumb to be greeted by Steve and Dianne Mills, former Californians, now from Georgia. They were there to crew for Pat McDonald, also doing his first hundred. They had plenty of hay and water and Redbird soon revived with their diligent care and so did I.

I arrived at Deadwood, not sure what help might be available. Some more people who I had met at the seminar were waiting for their rider; they were well-prepared with extra necessities and soon Redbird was ready for his check. This time we waited about twenty minutes for our turn. I was beginning to feel the time pressure. Although I was still okay, I had lost some of my extra margin of time. Fatigue had also begun to set in.

For me, mind drift is sometimes a problem after many hours of stress. An often unspoken facet of endurance riding is staying focused for long periods of time, as the shadow of fatigue waits just down the trail.

The help at Devil's Thumb and Deadwood was a key factor to our continuing in good spirits. Coming out of Deadwood Redbird was still alert and eager, wanting to catch the horses in front of him. We trotted through the long afternoon. The lowering sun's rays sifted down between the towering stands of pine trees. The heat, dust, and sounds of the horses' hooves clattering on the rocks blurred into one long steady feeling of endlessness. Yet, deep down, the will to finish drove us on. Sometimes we were alone, sometimes with other riders as I focused on getting to Michigan Bluff and seeing my crew again.

The trail became increasingly crowded as we reached the bottom of the canyon. People stopped to water their horses before beginning the long, arduous climb to the tiny village of Michigan Bluff. Now it seemed hotter than ever.

Tempers grew short as the riders strung out along the trail, walking, tailing, some wanting to trot...yet having no place to go. Even without checking my watch, I knew I was rapidly losing time. To complete the Tevis Cup one must complete the 100 miles in 24 hours. Twenty-four hours and one minute doesn't cut it.

There was nothing I could do except continue the journey, and concentrate on staying off the horse's back as much as possible.

At last, the welcome confusion at Michigan Bluff came into view. Climbing out of the canyon, I learned the meaning of *not much further, pretty soon* and *a mile or so,* as the riders questioned each other about the remaining distance to the top.

This stop was the highlight of the day. What first-class

treatment, and even a backrub! This is where I poured DMSO on my knees. We left the stop at 7:30, later than I had planned.

Redbird was in excellent shape. I felt encouraged on the way to Forest Hill, even as the shadows lengthened and the sun disappeared behind the mountains. When we reached the village, residents lined the street wishing us well. For a moment, I envied these people, all neat and clean, sitting on their porches. Then I reminded myself that I rode today by choice and someday I would have no choice but to sit on a porch and re-live these hours.

Although the vet check was very crowded I had incredible luck to be in the right place at the right time and went through quickly. It was 9:10 when I left Forest Hill. Now my worst fears were to be realized—riding in the dark!

Contrary to reports, there was no moon to guide us at first. The week before I had watched the moon's progress across the sky and knew approximately when it would appear. We continued to wind our way down the dark canyons toward the American River crossing, while glimpses of the moon encouraged me to believe it would soon appear above our heads.

I hoped to give myself some leeway by riding faster since Redbird seemed to get stronger and stronger. Dream on! The trail from Forest Hill to Francisco's, the next vet check, was another low point in the ride for me. This was when I realized that my riding skills were barely adequate for the task at hand.

I wondered if my fellow riders had kamikaze training, as we barreled down the hills through the dusty darkness. I had planned to trust Redbird's surefootedness and night vision to get us through. But my survival instincts prevailed and I slowed him down. Rider after rider passed us. Redbird became increasingly fretful and began to pull strongly. This was the worst incident with the snaffle bit, as Redbird and I struggled to be in control. Sometimes, unable to hold him any longer, I would let him go with the group. Then the fear of falling would seize me, driving me to briefly gain control again. We hurtled on in this nightmare of darkness, tears streaking my dust-blackened face.

As we reached Francisco's, I was on the edge of exhaustion. Although there was food and drink available, I had no time for it. I found someone to hold Redbird while I ran to the bathroom. It was now 12:10 a.m. Sunday morning and we only had 16 miles to go. I felt better about the time. Surely I could make it to Auburn before 5:00 a.m.

Intent on getting out of the vet stop, I took Redbird to be examined without checking his pulse. The vet listened to his heart and called to the scribe, "76." I was shocked because his pulse had come down so easily all day. In my haste, I forgot that a crew had worked on him at every stop.

As the vet examined him further, he heard congestion in Redbird's lungs. I felt that the congestion was caused by dust and was more concerned with getting his pulse down. I asked for a re-check since I still had a few minutes. Reluctantly, the vet agreed.

The young lady who had helped me earlier was standing nearby and jumped in to help. We began to use every technique we knew to lower his pulse. When I took him for a re-check, he was down to 58, more than meeting the criteria. I could tell the vet was still anxious to pull him so I suggested he take Redbird's temperature. I held my breath, knowing I had just played my last card. As we waited, it seemed that seconds ticked away so slowly. Finally we learned that the temperature was 101. I gave a great sigh of relief when the vet said, "Jog him out." And, I was free to go!

I had been held at Francisco's nearly an hour. I had no more time for errors. I knew I had to go for it, or the many hours Redbird and I had spent on the trail were for nothing. All my family and friends back East were pulling for me. I felt their thoughts and prayers stronger than ever, encouraging me to go on. If I could make it through the last vet check at 49 Crossing with no delay, I still had a chance.

When we reached the stop, I immediately found a helper and we went to work on Redbird. No delay. We left the stop at 3:15 a.m., only 15 minutes before cut-off time. I trotted away with the vet's parting words ringing in my ears, "You better hurry!" I knew these last few miles would be the longest in my endurance career.

We were now alone on the trail. Redbird paused in a moon-lit meadow to give a shrill whinny, listening intently for an answering call. Fortunately for me, he was smart. He knew he was the last horse and "home" was down the road. Thank goodness for the seminar which had enabled Redbird to be familiar with the trail.

The terrain had improved considerably and we trotted faster and faster toward our last landmark, No Hands Bridge. Even my fear of falling dimmed and I came to trust this horse completely to take me to the finish line.

The thought of not finishing overcame the pain, fatigue, and anxiety as we trotted and cantered through the pre-dawn hour.

The lights from the fairground shone like a beacon and then we entered the twisting trail through the last stretch of black woods. I closed my eyes, leaned over and grabbed his mane. As if he had been signaled, Redbird galloped to the finish line. As we burst out of the woods, I saw the lights at the timer's table. An incredible wave of relief swept over me…that "peaceful, easy feeling."

All the months, years and money I spent to live this moment were worth it, a thousand-fold. As I dismounted and leaned against Redbird's side, I knew this ride would forever be a highlight in my life.

Thanks California and Tevis volunteers for preserving this trail for future generations to enjoy. Thanks, too for all the wonderful people we met, for adding a new dimension to my life, and an even greater appreciation for the very special quality of endurance horses and their people.

Ann squeaked through the finish line with a mere five minutes to spare. She is eternally grateful to Redbird and says, "That was an amazing horse! I would have bought him and shipped him home if I could have."

Claire and Contessa

The Tevis Cup
Ann Cofield on Napoleon Redbird negotiating Cougar Rock

OVERSEAS

⇀The Land of the Beautiful Horses
Riding in Cappadocia, Turkey

The boarding call came over the loudspeaker: Istanbul. My plane was boarding for Istanbul, where I would catch a connecting flight to Kayseri, and then be picked up by the Akhal-Teke Horse Riding Center for my horseback trek in Cappadocia. My long-awaited dream of going to Turkey was finally being realized.

When I'd told people I was headed to Turkey, I got one of two reactions. One was "That's amazing! You are so lucky!" The other response was "Turkey? Why are you going to Turkey?" And the answer to that was, "Oh, for so many reasons!"

Turkey's unique location between Europe and the Middle East makes it unlike any other place on earth. One of the oldest continuously inhabited regions in the world, its history and geological formations render it a distinct destination. Turkey is the land of Homer, the cradle of so many religions, and an area of epic influence on the Greeks, the Romans, the world.

After a 10-hour flight, we began our descent into Istanbul. Lower and lower we dropped, and all we saw was water. Istanbul sits on a spit of land between the Black and Aegean Seas, and it began to appear as though we would be landing on one of those seas! Finally, just when we were all sure we were about to go for a swim, Istanbul appeared. Magical, mysterious, Istanbul.

Cappadocia is known throughout the world for its underground cities, unique rock formations, and ancient churches carved into hillsides and caves. Unlike many other places, travel in Turkey is experiential. Travelers are not removed from historic sites by endless miles of thick rope and barriers. They can walk inside, touch, and even sit on a structure from the 11th century. Antiquity in Turkey is just part of life.

For two decades I had dreamed of seeing the underground cities and unique geography, of viewing historical sites that I had only encountered in books. And what better way to do it than on horseback? The Akhal-Teke Horse Riding Center, located in Avanos, is uniquely situated in the heart of Cappadocia, just the region I wanted to see. Owned and operated by Ercihan Dilari, the center keeps a string of fit, forward going, and sure-footed horses that handle the terrain and long rides easily. Rides are available for everyone from beginners to the most experienced, but riders need to be sure to honestly state their riding experience in order to be matched with the appropriate mount and tour.

I had been introduced to the center by my friend, Susan Wirth. Susan had already taken several tours, and highly recommended it. I chose the Fairy Chimneys Tour, as it covered all the bases for what I wanted to experience in Turkey. It included a tour of an underground city, went right through many of the exquisite geographic formations, and took us to ancient historical landmarks. Some nights we returned to the center, spending the night in the charming Sofa hotel, while other nights were spent camping in surely the world's most unusual campsites, such as at the foot of a fairy chimney!

My riding partners included Elizabeth and Holly (a mother and daughter from Great Britain), Susan (from Massachusetts), and Ann (from New Zealand). Ann is clearly in love with both travel and horses. Her enthusiasm and energy were fabulous.

Ercihan seemed to be part of the landscape, so surely did he know every inch of it. Not only does he ride and train, but he has to be his own vet (with telephone help from a vet in Istanbul), farrier, and horse dentist. To run the type of establishment he has, and be out in the country so far from everything, he needs to be capable of doing just about anything the horses might need. Many times I awoke early to hear him tapping on a shoe that had come off.

Our rides ranged from leisurely walks with everyone chatting and snapping photos of the vistas and landscapes, to exhilarating gallops uphill to the top of a mesa.

Taste buds that have been napping for a lifetime awaken in Turkey. Fresh, vital, vibrant foods and flavors await you. The Turkish people do not tolerate bad food. From Turkey's volcanic soil springs a bounty of melons, grapes (there are vineyards everywhere in Cappadocia, sprouting from impossible substrates that resemble coarse gravel), tomatoes, cucumbers (with flavor!), beans, figs, limes, eggplant, pistachios, and orchards of peaches, pears, apples, and plums. On the remotest mesas with no signs of civilization in sight pumpkins and squashes grow everywhere. The sweetest blackberries in existence grow thick along the trails, the bushes overpopulated with deep, dark, luscious berries.

Every ounce of arable land is used in Turkey, and plenty of land that doesn't seem to have a remote possibility of being arable is used as well.

Lamb is a staple here, and chicken is very popular. But not chicken like you've ever known it. Cooked in a clay pot with tomatoes, onions, and potatoes, or over a campfire covered in a large metal can, it comes out moist and bursting with flavor. A favorite for all of us was böreg, a bit of cheese encrusted with phyllo dough and cooked to crispy perfection. It could be breakfast, it could show up as an appetizer at dinner, but it was always welcome!

Cappadocia means "land of the beautiful horses." The region was at one time known for its Akhal-Tekes, a hot-blooded breed native to Turkmenistan and descended from the now extinct Turkoman horse (believed to be one of the founding stallions of the Thoroughbred, the Byerley Turk). Akhal-Tekes are reputed to be the oldest domesticated breed of horse. Although currently the Akhal-Teke Horse Center primarily uses Arabian and Anatolian horses, plans are in the works to once again populate the barn with Akhal-Tekes.

Our horses were decked out in "Turkish bling," wearing beads around their necks, while my stirrups sported inlaid pink crystals. The center of the horses' beads contains an eagle, protecting them from harm.

The horses are incredibly fit, and reassuringly sure-footed. Much of the ground covered during the rides is either seemingly straight uphill, on footpaths barely wide enough for a deer edging steep canyons, or down treacherous slopes of loose sand and gravel. This is not a trip for the faint of heart. At one point our guide Ercihan points to the very high top of a mesa girded with sizable rock outcroppings. "We're going up there?" I gulp. What a surprise to reach the top and find it perfectly flat, farmed with hayfields and vineyards.

Turkey is a fabulous place to ride because of the freedom granted those on horseback. No fences hold riders in—or keep them out. It is wide open and horseback riders are allowed virtually anywhere, from open steppes and mesas to riverbanks and the cobblestone streets of villages. In the village of Mustafapasa (formerly an ancient Greek village known as Sinasos), we spotted an art museum as we were riding by. We all wanted to go in. No problem. Tying the horses in the street to whatever handy pole or post we could find, we trekked inside to view the exhibits. We were also treated to delicious pomegranate tea on a second story open tea room, where we had a beautiful view of much of the village.

Cars and trucks drove by the horses, but drivers and horses alike remained calm and unruffled.

Turkey emerged into the modern world thanks to its first president, Mustafa Kemal Atatürk, who recognized the country's need to leave behind the distant past it still clung to and bring itself into the 20th century. Atatürk distinguished himself in World War I during the infamous battle of Gallipoli, and then succeeded in creating a coalition to drive the occupying Allies out of the country. A new Republic of Turkey was formed on October 29, 1923, officially ending 623 years of Ottoman rule and government by the Sultan. Thanks to Atatürk, Turkey modernized their educational system and industry, and developed a secular, representative system of government, as well as established legal equality between the sexes. (Turkish women received the right to vote in 1934). An extensive rail network was also created during his 15-year rule.

One of Atatürk's many advances was a system of irrigation and drinking troughs throughout the country, which in practical terms allowed us the luxury of riding wherever we wanted without any worries about where to find water. Atatürk is idolized for his vision, for his ability to create a modern country that continues to grow and thrive today on the foundations he laid. Statues and pictures of him adorn villages and buildings throughout the country.

Five times a day, the call to prayer is heard in Turkey. It is a call that can be heard everywhere, no matter how remote the mesa or valley you may be in. The enigmatic sound is not only heard, but felt through its quavering vibration. There was no doubt: we were not in Kansas anymore.

The Turkish people are incredibly friendly and generous. Everywhere we went, villagers came out to bring us bunches of grapes from their vineyards (every house seems to come with its own personal vineyard), or apples for our horses, or fat red tomatoes that created instant bliss when eaten.

Part of the route we took ran along the Kizilirmak River, the longest river in Turkey. Dramatic vistas and ancient dwellings confront us at every turn. We visit Sarihan, a 13th century caravanserai (rest areas for camel caravans) located along the Silk Road. These "rest areas" were placed approximately every 80 kilometers along the Silk Road, with smaller ones halfway between.

The famed fairy chimneys of Cappadocia are truly amazing, *Lord of the Rings* come to life. Homes are created in fairy chimneys, and few things are more comical than a fairy chimney sporting a porch or a flowerbox. Part of our trip was spent camping, and one of our sites put our tents directly in the midst of a cluster of fairy chimneys. Cameras clicked all around, for who could imagine a more unique campsite anywhere?

Hot air balloons are tremendously popular in this area, and more than 100 balloons may be afloat at a time. Though it sounds crowded, there is little danger even if they bump into one another, and the sight of all the brilliantly colored balloons hovering over Cappadocia's unique topography is nothing short of spectacular.

Our many hours in the saddle required snacks to sustain us, and Turkey easily rose to the task. We would just nip into the endless small orchards and pick an apple, an apple-shaped, dimpled pear that tasted like nectar, a juicy, heavenly peach, plums, grapes, and walnuts. Tea breaks were also a treat, although many indulged in dark, sweet Turkish coffee.

We were well cared for throughout our journey by Serdar Tug and Mehmet Sibik, who met us at the campsites, bringing our luggage, setting up camp, and feeding us fabulous meals, including dinners cooked over the campfire. Serdar and Mehmet appeared to be mind readers, appearing with a cup of tea or a glass of wine, or whatever you were just thinking you needed to make everything perfect. I had been thinking about how nice it would be to lounge in a hammock toward the end of one ride; when we got to camp the first thing I noticed was a hammock strung between two trees!

I lived my dream of exploring an underground city when we visited Özkonak. It's astounding that these "cities" were carved out of stone, and provided everything necessary for living, such as ventilation, food storage, wine cellars, and water systems. As many as 3.500 people lived in the largest cities!

Two of the specialties of the village of Avanos, where we stayed, were pottery and Turkish rugs. Avanos has been a pottery center for 4,000 years, something I found hard to fathom coming from a country with a history of only a few hundred years.

We were treated not only to shopping expeditions for these area specialties, but a complete tour and education as to how they are created at local Bazaar 54. Ninety percent of Turkish rugs come from Cappadocia, where they are handmade locally with the colors and patterns varying according to the area. The rugs began as silk cocoons that were boiled to unravel a single filament, then the threads were dyed (with natural dyes from such items as walnut shells, mistletoe, and saffron), and then woven creating rugs in a huge range of colors and quality.

Fine silk rugs were literally works of art, with their lustrous sheen and colors that changed as we walked around them, much like the colors of the Grand Canyon. This method of creating rugs by hand from silk is a tradition that has continued for 5000 years.

The pottery, too, varied in quality depending upon whether it was ceramic, or quartz. But the colors were all brilliant. At Firca we were treated to the same education as we walked through the process of creating fine pottery. Some patterns are typical Turkish ones, while others are one of a kind, with the artist allowed free rein to his or her imagination.

We visited the Greek Orthodox monastery of Keslik, dating from the 9th and 11th centuries. Ancient frescoes graced the ceilings, and yet more ancient—Greek graffiti! The caves and tunnels went on endlessly and we embraced our inner children and ran amuck, exploring every room and cave we could get to.

A trip to a Turkish bath for a traditional "hamman" proved relaxing and beneficial to stiff muscles after hours in the saddle. Lying on heated tiles and being covered and massaged with oodles of bubbles was sublime; being rubbed vigorously with a rough cloth seemed just a bit too harsh.

On the final day we visited the open air museum of Göreme, a UNESCO World Heritage Site, consisting of a vast monastic complex with each monastery hosting its own rock-cut church. Stunning frescoes (some with the brilliant blue of lapis lazuli) graced the ceilings. These monasteries ranged from the 10th to the 12th centuries (hence the term "New Church" used at one point ironically meant one from the 12th century).

The only jarring note in a visit to Turkey was the litter. There appears to be no systematized approach to the pick up of garbage in the villages, and it is quite a distraction to see so much plastic packaging and other garbage in the streets, yards, and riverbanks, and marring the stunning landscape.

But don't let that stop you. Turkey is a land of spectacular vistas, amazing history, delicious food—and those beautiful horses. I'll be back.

The best times to ride in Turkey are the spring and fall (their seasons correspond to ours). The weather is generally warm, usually in the 70's during the day, but can get quite chilly at night. You do need a visa, but this can be obtained quickly and easily at the airport in Istanbul for $10. There are various rides available, many of them shorter, and some that don't require any camping. There are also activities available for non-riding partners. For more information on riding in Cappadocia, contact www.akhal-tekehorsecenter.com.

⤳ ICELAND

Thinking of taking a riding vacation? You're probably considering Ireland, or maybe Tuscany, Italy, or perhaps a cattle drive in Montana. But how about something really different?

Iceland is becoming an ever more popular destination for riders, with horse touring being one of the fastest growing businesses, and for good reason. This is a country with a concentration of one horse for approximately every three inhabitants.

Iceland is exotic. With a landscape so unlike any other that it was chosen as the place for the astronauts to practice their moon landings, Iceland will amaze you. On horseback you can cross highlands, ford rivers, view magnificent waterfalls and fjords, and see unspoiled nature at its best.

Language is not a problem, as almost everyone in Iceland speaks English. In this very hospitable country, the phone books are listed by first names!

There is only one type of horse you will ride on your Icelandic vacation, and that is the Icelandic Horse. (Okay, they are actually pony size, but don't ever call one a pony!) This is the only breed in the country, and the government keeps it that way, not allowing any imports in order to protect the health of the native horses. Once a horse leaves the country, it can never return home.

These sturdy, surefooted, muscular horses are not merely a stable ride over tough and uneven terrain; they are also delightful to sit on! Given your riding experience, you can get a "Steady Eddie" type, or you can get a speedy mount with a lot of spunk.

The weather in Iceland is changing constantly. Icelanders

joke that if you don't like the weather, don't worry—it will be different in five minutes. Outfitters always pack raingear so that you are prepared for any downpours.

Rides can be arranged at lengths varying anywhere from half a day to a week or more. Accommodations on these rides range from spartan to luxurious, but you can be sure they will always be clean. Often the footing for your rides will be lava rock from ancient (or perhaps, rather recent) volcanic explosions.

A good choice for a day ride is the "Hot Springs Ride." You will ride for half a day through some astounding scenery, including along the top of a canyon with waterfalls crashing down its sides. The ride takes a lunch break at a hot spring where you eat, change into a bathing suit, and soothe yourself with a relaxing soak before remounting and carrying on for the second half of the ride. (Changing can be a trick, as there are so few trees in Iceland. The country is so shy on trees, and the few that are around are so stunted, that the natives joke, "If you're lost in an Icelandic forest, what do you do?" The answer? "Stand up.")

The horses are small, but extremely sturdy, and capable of carrying big men with ease. The saddles are flat and quite comfortable.

Icelandic horses are three, four, or five-gaited. Their trademark gait, a tolt, is as comfortable as it gets and is very similar to the rack of the American Saddlebred. The tolt can be slow, or fast enough to keep pace with a galloping horse. The horses can maintain this gait for seemingly endless periods. At shows horses are often exhibited with riders holding full glasses of beer, never spilling a drop, proving just how smooth the horses are. Some horses also can pace, and racing pacing horses (astride, not in a sulky) is a favorite sport of Icelanders.

Learning to ride the tolt is a bit of a lesson in the universality of horsemanship. It's quite similar to dressage: one asks the horse to rock back, bring their hocks underneath them, and raise their front ends (although the head carriage is very different). What a charge! The horse surges forward in a smooth, powerful gait-you feel like you could sit it forever, ride forever.

When not riding, be sure to visit Reykjavik. This very European city boasts fine dining and great shopping. Go for a swim in one of the many beautiful public pools in the city. It doesn't matter what time of year it is. The pools are all geothermally heated. And if you're looking for a relaxing soak, there are hot tubs of varying degrees of heat: hot, hotter and hottest, lined up right next to each other.

Don't miss a chance to visit the Blue Lagoon. It alone is worth a visit to Iceland. It is another uniquely Icelandic experience, an odd combination of hedonism experienced in a a strongly prehistoric setting. Steam billows all around, as the hot water hits cool air. Lava walls surround you as you soak in the most relaxing mineral water in the world. Looking up, you wouldn't be the least surprised to see a pterodactyl winging its way overhead. When you emerge, the waters have stripped you of all stress and you are no more than a puddle of your former self.

The Blue Lagoon is quite close to Keflavik International Airport so it's easy to arrange a visit upon landing or on the way back for your return flight.

So, forget the commonplace. Try something different for this year's vacation. Experience Iceland. It's a vacation you'll never forget.

To check out Iceland, and Icelandic Horses for yourself, visit: www.horsesnorth.com.

⤳ Relief Riders International

A long-awaited vacation is approaching. On the one hand, you would like to take a scenic riding trip through an exotic land that you've always yearned to see. On the other hand, you would really love to give something back, perhaps build a house for Habitat for Humanity, or go to New Orleans to help rebuild America's most enigmatic city.

Relax, there's no need to make a choice. Now you can do both. With a company that combines exotic travel on horseback with humanitarian missions, Relief Riders International offers trips that provide food for the soul and light for the heart.

As a child, Relief Riders International founder Alexander Scouri attended a British military school in the foothills of the Himalayas. He tried many different activities at the school, including playing the piano, but the only thing that stuck with him was horseback riding. Alexander was a young boy separated by thousands of miles from his mother and his home in New York City. He found solace and peace in riding the native Marwari horses.

His life took many twists and turns, traveling the world, working in theatre and in special effects in movies. But, when his father and four close friends died in a two-month period, Alexander felt a need to realign his sense of direction and sense of self. He realized that there was more to life than what he was living. He wanted to give back, to provide an opportunity to help other people. The idea he came up with was simple, but elegant: ride across a beautiful country while helping others.

At the time, in 2003, the concept of "voluntourism" was unheard of. Yet, that was precisely what came to Alexander's mind. Alexander, whose father was Indian, returned to India to research and develop his idea in November 2003. When he returned, he told a friend "Hey, I'm working on this project—I'm going to ride horses through the desert and help people who need help. Poor people. Bring them medicine and food." The friend looked at him and said, "That's great. Why don't you call me when you wake up?"

It didn't stop Alexander, who knew intuitively that he would hit his mark. Since then, Alexander and Relief Riders International have completed over a dozen rides.

In conjunction with The Red Cross, Relief Riders International has developed far reaching medical and educational programs furnishing school supplies, goats, medical care, dental care, and cataract surgeries to rural communities in Rajasthan. The way they deliver these goods and services not only makes it unique, but also provides villagers with another dimension: entertainment. Doctors, dentists, and supplies come to town on horseback. Mounted on native Marwari horses (who were once considered divine and superior to all men) fitted in colorful, traditional tack, they create an entrance sure to capture everyone's attention.

In the United States, there is approximately one dentist for every 1500 people. In India those odds increase dramatically, to one in 90,000. Three-quarters of those dentists are located in urban areas, leaving rural populations desperately underserved. Living daily with a toothache is a common experience for many in India.

When Relief Riders arrive at a village, they set up a dental camp. While the dental team performs procedures, the Relief Riders work out of the camp dispensing toothpaste, toothbrushes, and education on dental hygiene.

"Goat's milk," according to the Journal of American Medicine, "is the most complete food known." In India, 48% of children under five suffer from malnutrition. Owning a goat can go a long way towards providing adequate nutrition for a family. And goats are easy to care for. Through the "Give a Goat" program, Relief Riders International has gifted goats to nearly 400 families.

The pediatric program, always a highlight of the rides, takes the staff to rural schools where they have the opportunity to meet and treat thousands of students. Riders are uplifted by the warm and heartfelt welcome from the children, inspired by their curiosity, and moved by the experience.

At one village, an infant only a few months old was brought in with a life-threatening laceration and infection. The baby was treated and the parents were given antibiotics to continue treatment. The baby would have died if not for the Relief Riders' program. It is precisely this kind of incident that makes the rides so transformative for participants.

Some people express finding their careers revitalized, others have found deeper levels in their personal relationships, and there are those for whom the experience served to kick-start a life changing dream project. Almost all of them have been inspired to continue to help others.

Alumni Rider Andrew Mersmann describes his experience of the relief ride as "a breakthrough that just picks you up and puts you down somewhere exponentially further along the road than you expected to get." Inspired by his experience, Andrew returned home with a new perspective and within 12 months manifested a beautiful and purposeful book project, Frommer's *500 Places Where You Can Make a Difference*. Alexander finds the experience appeals to a wide variety of travelers, describing them as "a group of wildly interesting people with a common purpose." He has had people who haven't ridden in 25 years participate. The ride reignited a long dormant passion in many, coupling it with a chance to give back, and to positively impact the communities visited.

Relief Riders International may seem like a small organization, with a limited number of rides, but its impact has been so dramatic that it was named the recipient of the 2010 United Nations NGO Positive Peace Award in the small business category. This award honors and recognizes organizations positively impacting their communities through corporate responsibility. Alexander keeps the rides small so that he can remain personally connected to them. There are no plans for large, "mass produced" rides. To date 20,000 people have been treated by Relief Riders International.

Although making such an impact is more than enough reward in its own right, the trips provide breathtaking scenery unlike anything else one can experience on earth. Days are spent riding the majestic Marwari horses through cinematic desert landscapes. Overnights take place in ancient forts and beautiful camps. The vibrant terrain of southern Rajasthan offers a wealth of varied experiences from sleeping in a serene desert oasis to joining villagers in a jubilant celebration of Holi (the festival of colors), to riding through a moonscape terrain by moonlight. During the day, indigenous wildlife such as black buck, desert foxes, and blue bulls are spotted.

A new itinerary winds itself around the stunning Aravelli mountain range, taking riders from the lakeside Sardar Samand fort to Kumbalgarh. This 3300 foot mountain range offers unparalleled vistas of the Thar Dersert. Kumbalgarh boasts the world's second longest wall (22 miles), built in the 15th century to protect its people.

The year 2011 marked Relief Riders International's expansion into Turkey. New programs are in the works, and the company worked closely with local officials and citizens in the Cappadocia region to build children's playgrounds in towns that needed them. The playgrounds have been a huge hit with the kids!

Located in the middle of Turkey, Cappadocia (a UNESCO World Heritage Site), is known for its fine horses and natural wonders. The high plateau of Anatolia, with its colorful river valleys, dramatic ravines, and volcanic peaks, served as the backdrop to the Turkish journey, which took place from June 17-29, 2011.

A brilliant vision has grown into a source of hope for thousands of people, and a chance for the experience of a lifetime for hundreds more.

(If you would like to take part in a ride, or would like more information, contact Relief Riders International: www.reliefridersinternational.com.)

⎯⁀ PIYE

The love of horses goes back to the most ancient of times, to the beginnings of civilization.

For five centuries, Egypt had been in a steady decline. After the brilliant and enduring rule of Ramses the Great, succeeding pharaohs ruled poorly. In time, the priests seized power and Egypt continued its decline. Neighboring Libya took advantage of Egypt's weakness, invading and declaring their leaders as the new kings.

Soon Egypt was so weak that it found itself with five feuding factions, each declaring itself the true pharaoh of the country.

At this point, Egypt's southern neighbor Nubia (where modern Sudan is now located) turned its attention to the ailing country. Egyptians referred to the Nubians as the Kush, most often the "Vile Kush." For thousands of years the Kush had been under Egypt's thumb. Now, Piye, who had united the tribes of Nubia, marched north and conquered Egypt.

Piye was not there to grab the spoils of war. Saddened by the deplorable depths the country had sunk to, Piye went to re-establish the noble tradition of Egypt, to return it to its greatness.

The in-fighting between the factions had resulted in fear and uncertainty among the regions' peoples, and an all time low in the state of the country. But it was one result of this fighting that in particular incensed Piye.

The ruler had a real soft spot for one thing: horses. His love for horses was legendary. When he went to the royal stables (now *his* royal stables) he was shocked at the condition of the horses, at the mistreatment they had been subject to. They had not been properly fed or cared for. The former ruler, Nemrod, was promptly punished for his mistreatment of the royal horses.

Piye's words, and passion, are preserved for posterity. On his victory "stela" (an upright stone or slab with an inscribed surface) his impassioned voice resonates clearly from the past. "I swear, as Ra loves me, that on my heart weighs more the fact that these horses have suffered hunger, than all the damages you've (Nemrod) done for your ambitions."

Ann on Kelibah, which means Butterfly,
Kelibeh is an Arabian former racehorse

Turkey

Camping by a fairy chimney

Camping in front of a cave dwelling

The entrance to an underground city

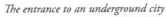

Iceland

A Relief Rider to the rescue in India

The architecture in India is astonishing.

AND MORE

↷ Not Something You See Everyday

By Robert Goodman

Purim is the Jewish holiday described in the biblical Book of Esther. The story celebrates the Jewish victory over their Babylonian enemies, especially the death of the wicked Haman, royal vizier to King Ahasuerus, through the miraculous efforts of Queen Esther, her older cousin Mordechai who raised her, and the "hidden face of God."

Each March since 2006, in an effort to make the Purim story come alive, Rabbi Shmuel Herzfeld of Ohev Sholom, "The National Synagogue," in Washington, D.C., has reenacted the Purim story on the city streets. This fun and festive day is growing by leaps and bounds every year, as Mordechai dressed in King Ahasuerus' royal robes is led on a horse by the wicked Haman to the delight of children who gain a better understanding of the biblical story.

The parade route is along the very cosmopolitan Connecticut Avenue to K Street NW, famed for its lobbyists and lawyers. There is a police escort followed by a small klezmer band leading the parade in front of Haman leading Mordechai on the horse. Trailing the parade are jugglers, a stilt walker, a unicycle rider, and dozens of parade goers dressed in festive costumes spinning "groggers" (noise makers). Hamentashen, a triangle-shaped cookie usually wrapped around a fruit or chocolate filling, are given to the many parade watchers. It's all quite a sight to see, especially for the non-Jewish onlookers who are unfamiliar with the Purim story.

Ohev Sholom's second Purim parade was scheduled, permits acquired, and the day was fast approaching. I had ridden as "Mordechai" the previous (first) year, and Rabbi Herzfeld asked me to ride again this year. He knew that I had been riding for many years and would feel comfortable enough to ride a horse safely in the middle of the very busy traffic. I was asked to find a new horse for this second parade, a white horse if possible as that would look more regal. I asked a friend for help and was led to Rick Jones and Marcia Brody, owners of Carriages of the Capital, and their friendly white Percheron-cross carriage horse named Blizzard. Blizzard's other job is leading South Asian grooms in for their traditional weddings.

Sunday, March 4th, 2007, started out as a chilly and windy day. The parade route this year went from near the White House to the United States Capitol Building, nearly one and a half miles from 15th Street NW to 3rd Street NW along Pennsylvania Avenue. Due to the cold weather there were hardly any parade watchers along the route.

The parade was fun, loud, and well attended by at least 60 costumed adults and children from Ohev Sholom. Everyone stopped to take photographs with Blizzard and Mordechai at the end of the parade. There was one group picture taken with the U.S. Capitol in the background, a very historic picture. All the parade goers cleared the area within five minutes of the end of the parade. The only ones who remained were Marcia, Blizzard, a friend of mine, and me.

The sun had come out and it took the nip out of the cold air. I suggested to Marcia that we walk Blizzard to his trailer and we to our vehicles on the pea gravel walkway of the National Mall so that we did not have to contend with the passing car on Pennsylvania Avenue. No sooner had we taken our first steps when a red, white, and blue Washington, D.C. Metropolitan Police car speedily drove up from behind us with lights flashing, siren blaring, and a voice coming from within the police car telling us to immediately stop where we were and present our identifications.

There we were, three humans and one gigantic white horse,

all dressed in unusual costumes. I was wearing a long white beard, a golden jeweled crown, and carrying just as regally as I could the train of my long purple robe in my right hand and a bucket of horse manure in my left. Marcia was wearing her English riding habit. Blizzard was dressed in his colorful beaded South Asian wedding neck collar with matching headdress and jingling sleigh bells around his neck. My friend was carrying a short-handled shovel.

Out from the police car stepped a very short police officer that did not look the least bit happy to see us. "Please show me your ID's," he said rather sternly and officially. We looked at each other and said as politely as we could to the police officer that we had left our identification in our respective vehicles. Who knew we'd need them? We explained to the police officer that we had just finished our Purim parade, that we were walking the horse and ourselves back to our respective vehicles, and that we felt it would be a much nicer walk back on the National Mall. The police officer then said with little compassion or care for our comfort, "You'll have to get off the Mall."

I respectfully asked the police officer why we had to leave the Mall. He explained that all private horses were banned from the National Mall as a means to prevent the spread of possible infection to the National Park Services' Park Police horses. As Marcia and I were familiar with extremely infectious equine diseases, we immediately understood and told the police officer we would get off the National Mall ... just as quickly as we could. Thankfully, we were not fined nor arrested, but these thoughts did pass through our minds. This would have been a most unfitting ending to a joyous Purim celebration. (I later learned from a National Park Police mounted officer that the only reason we would have been required to leave the National Mall grounds was if we did not have the correct parade permit papers to walk a horse on the National Mall grounds. Since I did not personally possess the parade permits on me, it was a moot point. We left the Mall immediately.)

As we proceeded to 4th Street, the next cross street along the National Mall, I turned to the police officer to ask one last question. "How did you know we were on the Mall?" Without skipping a beat, the police officer responded, "We received a dispatch that there was a 'king walking a white horse on the Mall.'"

We could not stop laughing at this remark. We imagined what the dispatcher must have heard, and imagined that the dispatcher must have asked the caller to repeat the message when the call came in from the busybody with a cell phone who felt the need to report our apparent violation of the law. "That's right, 'A king walking a white horse on the Mall.'" After all, it's not something you see everyday.

ERIK

Driving down a street one day, Jack Gordon spied a sign. "Horse for Sale" it read. He stopped to investigate.

Actually, there were two horses for sale. The first one was a typey brown Thoroughbred, a beautiful horse. The second one was a huge chestnut horse with lots of chrome. Although pretty, he had a big ugly scar on his leg and a miserably short tail.

Jack had stopped to buy a horse for his daughter. Twelve-year-old Linda had been taking riding lessons for long enough. It was time for her first horse.

But Linda was unimpressed with the big chestnut and she hated his tail. She had fallen immediately in love with the gorgeous brown Thoroughbred (*who had a great tail*). Besides, Linda at that point measured a scant four feet. What did she want with a 17 hand high horse?

Jack was unmoved by his daughter's reaction. "We're buying the chestnut," he told her. Linda burst into tears.

Erik went home to live with them. The picture was ludicrous, the petite child on the huge horse. Jack had to give his daughter a leg up every time she rode as there was no way she could reach the saddle on her own. But Erik's inner beauty started to show through. He taught Linda everything. She learned to jump, showed in pleasure and hunter hack, and took up fox hunting.

Fox hunting proved to be one of Erik's specialties. He and Linda followed the hounds with Spring Valley Hunt in New Jersey. Erik loved to gallop cross-country and jump the numerous post and rail fences and coops, carrying Linda safely over the big, solid jumps.

He took care of his little girl, growing to know her voice, to learn his name.

When the big Thanksgiving Day hunt approached, Linda became very excited. She had dreamed of participating in it; now that dream was coming true. Held at a huge estate in wealthy New Vernon, this hunt was a special tradition in the area, and Linda felt a sense of awe when they arrived. She was actually going to be riding in it.

The estate gave off the air of an English country manor with its verdant fields and stone courtyard. Over 50 people turned up to ride in this memorable event, and to partake of the fabulous hunt breakfast that followed. The master-of-hounds, decked out in a blue shadbelly, rode side-saddle, while Alex Foreman, a top judge, served as whipper-in for the hounds.

As a drag hunt, people could follow along in their cars on the road and watch. Jack came, thrilled to see his daughter participate in this prestigious event. Things started out well, with Erik and Linda dashing across fields, easily clearing the fences, both of them exhilarated with the sport. But as they raced along a narrow path between two fields, they came to a huge coop at the top of the hill. Erik slid to a stop.

Following hunt protocol, Linda and Erik went all the way to the back of the line, behind scores of horses. They approached the fence again. Again Erik stopped, this time dumping Linda. Horrified, Linda's father jumped out of the car, and hurried up the hill. Out of shape and a heavy smoker, his progress was slow and laborious.

Erik, freed of his rider, took off flat out across the fields, his tail straight up in the air like a flag. He galloped two full fields away from Linda, catching up with the rest of the hunt.

Unhurt, Linda jumped to her feet, fuming. Hardly cutting an imposing figure, the little girl, hands on her hips, yelled to the big horse in a commanding voice, "ERIK!! You come back here!" Outrage was evident in her tone.

Erik heard the high-pitched voice demanding his return. To everyone's surprise, he obeyed! Turning in his tracks, he took off at a flat gallop back in Linda's direction.

He came back to Linda, and he never stopped at a fence again.

He continued to take care of Linda and became the best first horse anyone could have. The best horse Linda, who has had many horses at the top in the zone or the country, ever had. The red horse with the ratty tail that she didn't want turned into the best horse *ever*.

⟶ The Proposal

Scott Tarter had been dating Elizabeth Rohfritch for three and a half years. As Scott says, "It took me a while to figure out how to convince her."

Liz and Scott met at Claremont Riding Academy in New York City in December, of 2000, when Scott arrived to pick up some horses. While other people play golf, or tennis, or ride on the weekends, Scott drove horse vans for NYCONN, ferrying horses back and forth to shows. Although Scott had a good "suit job" in the city, and lived on East 85th Street, he drove vans so he could stay in touch with horses.

As he put down the ramp on the van on West 89th Street, Liz came out of the barn. It was their first glimpse of each other. Scott was bleary-eyed from his long early morning round-trip to the NYCONN yard in Brewster to pick up the van. Liz remembers thinking, "There's our driver. I hope he speaks English."

After the horses were loaded, Scott drove the van north on 684 towards River Run Farm in Brewster, where the horses would show. As he approached Exit 8, very near his destination, Liz called. She addressed Scott as "Steve."

The minivan Liz was driving had died near Exit 18 (coincidentally, the same exit as Twin Lakes Farm, perhaps a glimpse into the future?) on the Hutchinson River Parkway. Could Scott come get her?

"No," Scott answered, he couldn't.

Liz didn't take it well, despite Scott's attempt to explain that horse vans are not allowed on, and do not fit on, the Hutchinson River Parkway. No one would have guessed then that anything good would come out of this.

Yet here it was, March of 2004, and they had been seeing each other for years. Liz was working at Sleepy Hollow Country Club, and had been asked by Pat Neff of Twin Lakes Farm in Bronxville, New York, to judge a schooling show.

Pat was away in Virginia, but had agreed that Scott could use her facility as the site for his proposal to Liz. Scott had also secured the cooperation of the announcer, Hilary, trainer Emily Bodion, and office manager Carol Dussault. Between the four of them, they arranged a scenario that Scott had hatched while watching *Meet the Parents*. In this scene, Ben Stiller's "Greg" arranges for his girlfriend's (schoolteacher "Pam") students to hold signs up outside her classroom, asking her if she will marry "Greg."

Liz was judging the last class in the indoor arena, the final class of the day. The riders were lined up in the middle of the ring at the conclusion of the flat class. Due to the orchestrations of Hilary, Emily, and Carol, letters were pre-printed on the back of the riders' numbers. The riders did not line up randomly. They formed rank in a very specific order.

Liz looked at the numbers, and then looked at her card. As her head was down, the riders were signaled, and they flipped their numbers over. The cards on their backs now spelled out, "Liz, Will You Marry Me?"

However, Liz neglected to look up again. She continued to stare at her card. Hilary prompted her to look the numbers over one more time.

Liz, exhausted after eight hours of multiple walk-trot sections and other endless lower level classes, replied curtly. But she finally looked up and began with "Who messed with my numbers?"

Scott crossed the ring and stopped a few feet away from the rail. Liz walked from the viewing area and met Scott in the arena. He got down on one knee and proposed. Liz didn't say yes immediately, perhaps in a bit of shock. "There was some negotiation, a giggle of laughter, and then a smile," Scott recalls.

But the answer was ultimately "Yes."

It was the beginning of an entirely new life for both of them. Six months later, they signed a contract to purchase Twin Lakes Farm from Pat Neff, who was retiring. In 2007 their first daughter was born, on Pat's birthday. She is named Allison Patricia after Pat Neff.

In 2008, during the July 24th USEF horse show at Twin Lakes, during the Children's Hunter Horses, Liz and Scott were most notably absent. They were in the hospital welcoming Emily Carol Tarter into the world. The horse show stopped when the announcement was made that the new baby was here. But no name was announced: the proud parents wanted to introduce Emily Carol to Carol Dussault personally before the announcement of her namesake was made. Liz and Scott are always grateful to Pat as it was she who allowed Scott to propose in her indoor and started the whole family.

~~·) CHESTNUT MARES

C hestnut mares have a reputation, often well earned, to uphold. Just like redheads, they're presumed hot, with fiery tempers. So when I saw the chestnut mare jigging into the ring, the whites of her eyes showing, with a rookie child rider on her back, I saw disaster headed in my direction.

Judging is not an easy job. Not only does a judge have to sort out the different placings, but this has to be done quickly, while insuring the safety of those within your ring. This means that sometimes a canter must be ended abruptly before you've really had a chance to choose the ribbon winners, in order to prevent a horse from building up a head of steam. Safety is always the utmost priority, particularly with children's classes.

The pair somehow survived the flat classes. The rider, although short on experience, had a measure of tact that helped keep the lid on the mare. And the mare, although she would quicken, never quite reached the boiling point, which allowed me to keep the class rolling and do my job.

Alas, despite my fervent hope to the contrary, the mare was entered in an over fences class. It was a simple, twice around the outside, course for maiden riders. Perfect for the mare to gather speed unfettered by a turn or change of direction.

Miraculously the pair proceeded down the first line with both horse and rider emerging intact. After turning and cantering across the short side at the bottom of the ring, they headed for the line up the other long side. As soon as they made the turn I sensed trouble. There was an unsettling look in the rider's eye.

"*Oh oh!*" She was going to gun it. And she did. Kicking

the mare and flinging her elbows wildly, the rider saw a distance a mile away and asked the horse to go for it. The mare, obligingly enough, took off from the faraway distance.

The rider did not.

Royally left behind, she was thrown out of the saddle and landed off to the right, still on the horse but only because her arms were tightly wrapped around the mare's neck.

A gasp went up through the crowd, and, I have to admit, my voice was among them. I have a rule. No one gets hurt in my ring. I don't like to see my rule broken, and it looked like such an occurrence was imminent.

The rider screamed in terror as the pair continued down the line. There was no way she would be able to hold on over the next fence.

Then a hush fell over the terrified crowd. To everyone's amazement, the mare slowed her freakish pace. Veering gently off to the side of the jump, the horse slowed gradually to a halt. The mare then gently shoved her right shoulder back, boosting her young rider back into the saddle.

Rider and horse were safe. The audience resumed breathing.

"You better thank your horse," a spectator told the rider as they exited the ring. "She saved you."

The girl nodded and hugged the mare's neck.

I should know better than to stereotype. We are all individuals, whether human or horse.

⟶ WAR HORSE

Not even war can separate a man from his beloved horse.

Alfred first meets Joey as a frightened foal who has just been weaned from his mother. Their relationship begins with a bribe. Frustrated that Joey will not come near him, Alfred resorts to the age-old trick of rustling some grain in a bucket. Thus begins a bond that lasts a lifetime.

Alfred's father, Ted, purchased Joey at auction for a lofty price. Paying for the foal with the money for the mortgage, he incurs the wrath of his wife Rose. But Alfred is enchanted.

Alfred takes over the care and training of Joey. A Thoroughbred/draft cross, Joey is destined to be a hunter, not a farm horse. He is highly opinionated and as he grows he is happy to carry Alfred through the fields, but feigns terror at the sight of a harness yoke.

But Joey's home depends on him learning to pull a plow, and in the end he gives in. This is fortunate, because that training later saves his life.

World War I intrudes in the life of the farmers. Joey's father, tempted by a large sum of money offered by the army, sells Joey off to be an officer's horse. Alfred and his mother are outraged; Alfred is heartbroken at the loss of his best friend.

World War I is no place for the cavalry. The play pays homage to the millions of horses who died senselessly in this war. The horses face machine guns, barbed wire, and tanks. Under such conditions, they are powerless, and die tragic deaths.

Joey survives initially because, as a hunter, he jumps the barbed wire instead of becoming helplessly entangled in it like so many others. Captured by the Germans, he comes under the protection of a horse-loving officer. The fact that Joey is broke to harness (much to the surprise of the Germans) saves his life, as he is given a job where he does not have to enter battle, but instead pulls the ambulance.

Alfred, still too young to join the army, runs away and enlists in order to find Joey and bring him home safely. Life isn't life without Joey, and Alfred is willing to risk his own in order to save his horse.

War Horse, while chronicling the bond between a horse and his human, also explores the timeless link between horses and humanity, for in the end it is Joey who unites the enemies. War Horse speaks to the travesty of war, and the commonality between all humans (the Germans in War Horse are just like their English "enemies": some kind, some evil, and most wondering why they are in the midst of this terrifying war and what its purpose is).

Joey causes much consternation when he does end up snared by barbed wire, in no man's land. Both sides are heartbroken by the horse's suffering, and want to help him, but fear reprisal from the enemy should they reach out. Their desire to save a horse causes a ceasefire to be called and the enemies work side by side to free him. Communicating with hand gestures, they free Joey and find peace between them. A coin is tossed to see who gets to keep the horse.

The English win, and take the limping horse to a vet to get patched up. Although Alfred is at the same location as Joey, he cannot see him due to being blinded by tear gas. Joey, however, hears his Alfred and crosses the hospital yard to reach him, and snuffle in his ear.

The war ends, and Alfred, after nursing Joey back to health, rides triumphantly home to his family.

The puppets are amazing, the play is poignant yet funny, and it tells a beautiful story about the love of a man and a horse.

Rob on Blizzard at the Capital

Erik

The Proposal

We apologize if you tried to reach us on the loveofthehorse@sbcglobal.net address. We got so spammed that we had to discontinue using it. If you have a story to share let us know! Stories can be about any breed or discipline, but must be funny, inspirational, or informational.

If you have a story to share or would like to contact the author, you can reach us at annjamieson23@gmail.com.

Photo: Debbie T. Kilday

ANN JAMIESON

Ann Jamieson is a United States Equestrian Federation Judge licensed in hunters, jumpers, and hunt seat equitation. She shows her two Thoroughbreds, Fred Astaire and The Virginian, in hunters and dressage, and looks forward to competing in hunter derbies.

Ann has written numerous articles for magazines and newspapers. She currently writes for "Today's Equestrian" magazine.

This is Ann's fourth volume of *For the Love of the Horse*.

Ann shares her Kent, Connecticut home with two Ocicats, Oliver and Chester.